Cross Stitch:
Inspirations
~ in Color ~

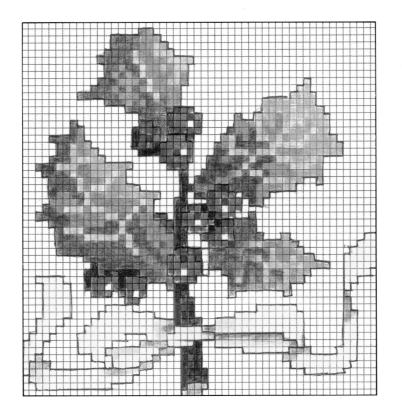

More Than 100
Exquisite Designs

Designs by Miky Dessein
Photography by Elio Michelotti
Text by Elda Filippa and Mariarosa Schiaffino

FRIEDMAN/FAIRFAX
PUBLISHERS

CONTENTS

A FRIEDMAN/FAIRFAX BOOK

© 1992 Idealibri. s.t.d.
© 1995 Michael Friedman Publishing Group, Inc.

Library of Congress Cataloging-in-Publication Data

Punto croce. English
   Cross stitch: inspirations in color.
      p.   cm.
   ISBN 1-56799-195-5
   1. Cross—stitch—Patterns.   I. Title.
TT778.C67C77313   1995
746.44'3041—dc20
                                    94-35668
                                       CIP

Originally published in Italian as *Punto Croce*

Translation by Marietta Rossetto
Designed by Miky Dessein

Printed in China by Leefung-Asco Printers Ltd.

All photographs were taken at Romantek Hotel, Turm at Fie
allo Sciliar (Bolzano) and in the Maison Rose at
Eugenie-les-Bains (France).

Photography by Elio Michelotti

For bulk purchases and special sales, please contact:
Friedman/Fairfax Publishers
Attention: Sales Department
15 West 26th Street
New York, New York 10010
212/685-6610 FAX: 212/685-1307

PREFACE

"If you know how to sew on a button you know how to embroider a rose." Whoever formulated such an encouraging assertion must have been referring to cross stitch. This book aims to prove the truth of this statement.

A cross stitch is a tiny, tiny stitch with widespread fame today. It is a form of embroidery that requires simple patience and yet gives extraordinary results and can be learned from the pages of this book. It is a temptation that is difficult to resist because its main appeal stems from its "scholastic method" approach which sets out the instructions in a manner that ensures easy, accurate mastery of the necessary skills.

At one point in history, experienced needleworkers were available to pass on their skills to others. There existed an oral tradition of easy, spontaneous words and gestures through which the craft was passed on to beginning stitchers.

Today, must we renounce this tradition because life is too hectic and rushed? No. This book aims to encourage cross stitch, a craft that is easier to discover and rediscover than one might imagine. It is not only a wonderfully meditative hobby but also one that provides a satisfying link with the past. The chapter sequence found here presents a beautiful story of embroidery, enhanced with scintillating color, subtle shading, and carefully selected designs.

We are convinced that the revival of this craft will be a story with a happy ending.

INTRODUCTION

*C*ross stitch, always one of the most popular forms of embroidery, has lately gained an even larger following. This recent surge of interest may be due in large part to the fact that while the technique itself is relatively easy to master, the results can be breathtaking.

Even with the hectic pace of life today, would-be embroiderers will find cross stitch a wonderfully doable craft. Most projects are of a size that is easily portable—allowing you to stitch at various moments during the day—and even a few minutes' work each day will yield a finished piece in a surprisingly short time.

Color plays a major role in determining the beauty of an embroidered piece, so the chapters of this book have been divided by color—and great care has been given to the choice of threads for each project—to ensure stunning results even for beginning stitchers.

Whether a beginner or an experienced cross stitcher, you'll find Cross Stitch: Inspirations in Color *the perfect cross-stitch resource—one you'll refer to for years to come as a limitless source of fresh design inspiration.*

COLOR HARMONY
IN CROSSED THREADS

Traditionally, white is the color of household linens. Color, however, has always been used to brighten and enliven home decor. Color also plays a leading role in cross stitch.

Cross stitch is a technique that was the most popular and widely used embroidery stitch of the last century. This genial craft was first used in Germany in 1804 and contributed, in a very significant fashion, to the development of associated stitches such as Continental stitch, half stitch, and tent stitch. Today, cross stitch is enjoying a renewed popularity so keen that it is considered a "phenomenon" at the center of the revival of traditional handicrafts in general and embroidery in particular. The reasons for this enthusiasm probably lie in the easy execution of the craft and its extremely appealing decorative impact.

Cross stitch is easier to do than to say. It is geometrical, regular, and simple to follow, and uses the fabric count of loosely woven material such as canvas. You simply stitch twice in diagonal directions, crossing one stitch over the other. It is often called square stitch because of its basic structure and also because cross-stitch designs are usually drawn on graph paper—every square represents a stitch, making the precision of the craft extremely easy to master and original designs, faces, and motifs easy to create.

With color and tone it is possible to create greater clarity of design and a three-dimensional effect similar to that of tapestry. In needlework dating from the seventeenth and eighteenth centuries, the shadings of color are, generally speaking, more subdued. This is not solely due to fading over time but rather to a widespread interest in light colors—the harmony and effect of tone on tone or on a number of restricted tints gave a very refined look to decorations. In the nineteenth century, especially in the second half, the discovery of aniline dye, which was used in the industrial world to dye yarn, created a whole range of tints that were much richer in tone. This change in color appreciation spread to embroidery, and the craft adopted the use of stronger colors and contrasts that were a far cry from the tonal qualities of the previous century.

Today, naturally, chemical advances and nature itself provide us with an infinite array of yarns and threads of various colors and tints. A wider range of colors now makes almost any design possible. A few base colors, various tones of one color, or, in a completely opposite manner, a multitude of tints and gradations can be used to give masterly shading or a particular effect to an embroidered piece.

This book has chosen to highlight the theme of colored thread—from rose to green, from yellow to blue, to red, to violet, to orange—and the array offers a myriad of ideas and suggestions.

We have developed the theme of color liberally, encompassing flowering vine shoots and wreaths, baskets of fruit, bunches of flowers tied with ribbons, and, embracing the classical notion of the garden, the vegetable patch, the orchard, and the countryside. This naive aspect of nature is an inspirational theme for embroidery motifs. There are also other traditional motifs in cross stitch that have been reinterpreted in modern style: the letters of the alphabet and the numbers used in samplers or in beginners' works on which the young embroiderer learned the art of sewing as well as the skills of reading, writing, and arithmetic.

Geometric and stylized motifs are presented as center-pieces, borders, and frames, offering another outlet for creativity and personal expression.

The photographed works are set out in planned designs that are easy to follow—sometimes a single motif, but more often, a repeated pattern forming a border. Many additional designs on various themes are set out in chart form only. Another significant feature of the designs is that for each, the number of required stitches and the measurement according to the chosen fabric are given. This information is extremely practical for anyone about to begin embroidery because the actual dimensions are already calculated and the process of adapting a design is clearly explained.

Therefore you can choose the stitches, the season, and the desired color of thread. Our wish is that cross stitch will be for you as it was for the passionate devotee who claimed that "Embroidery is happiness created."

Mariarosa Schiaffino

Inspirations in
ROSE

*O*ptimism, confidence, benevolence, sweetness—no other color evokes such a positive vision of life as the rose-colored thread used in embroidery. The statistics confirm this: in dinner settings for the table, in personal linen, and in the bedroom, rose is the favorite color worldwide. A calm color born of the mixture of red (aggressive and dynamic) with white (innocent and peaceful), it gathers the striking clarity of the former by warming the coolness of the latter.

There is no aspect of this color that can be viewed negatively. It is the aura of dreams, love stories, and tenderness. Even nature expresses its most gentle and benign self through the color rose—the flush of a baby's cheeks, the fullness of a peach, the transparent coral *pelle d'angelo*, the exquisite flesh of salmon and shrimp.

The finest creation of the color rose is the beautiful flower, queen of the gardens, which takes its name from the color (or is it vice versa?) and displays it in all its most enchanting shades. The floral world is bursting with pink: the magnificent peony, the subtle azalea, the gentle periwinkle (clematis), the wild heather, and a thousand other species. It is for this reason that the color rose is featured so often in embroidery: corollas, buds, and rosy petals spread across the linen, gathering close in bunches and cascading in garlands.

*A*bove and detailed on page 11: The floral border is the undisputed central feature of cross-stitch embroidery. It is the "patchwork motif" normally indicated on a design with letters or arrows. Most patchworks include a border that is useful for decorating long strips such as the edge of a sheet, the outer edge of a quilt, the bottom of a curtain, or the edge of a tablecloth. On this border, the toned colors merge into the clear woven surface of the fabric, which is almost an antique white.

*R*ight: These little square gardens enhance a tablecloth and are linked together with a white latticework decorated with a subtle green creeper. This combination can decorate the table surface and the fall of the tablecloth, and can have countless variations because there are no limits to geometric possibilities— chess board patterns, zigzags, diagonal designs, and so on. It is always best to plan the design before beginning, sketching it out in proportion on graph paper with precise measurements.

*L*eft: To speak of cross stitch without referring to samplers, or first attempts, is overlooking the full story. This is a delightful first attempt with a delicate union of initials and numbers, flowers around the border, and nongeometric shapes— almost an album of designs that can be consulted when looking for inspiration for a picture frame, a finishing touch, or a border (See pp. 24–25.)

*A*bove: Another border design, which makes ingenious use of the bands of cross stitch continuing outside the nosegays and links them together to give life to this very beautiful American design. Light yellow (or another pale color) can be used for the bands; soft pastel tones ranging from rose to red, green, or light blue for the flowers. Note that the more you increase the number of threads per 4 inches, the smaller the embroidery design. (See pp. 22–23 and p. 98.)

bove and right: Bring color to a subtly checked tablecloth. Choose a sophisticated gray check for the fabric. For the flowers and leaves, use the full range of the deeper shades of rose, and sprinkle the green with yellow. Vary the flowers and use cross stitch for the blooms, outlining each flower in backstitch. Work flower motifs in backstitch only for airy fill-in motifs.

THE DESIGNS

Inspirations in Rose

* The color numbers of all the designs in this book
refer to the DMC Embroidery Floss.

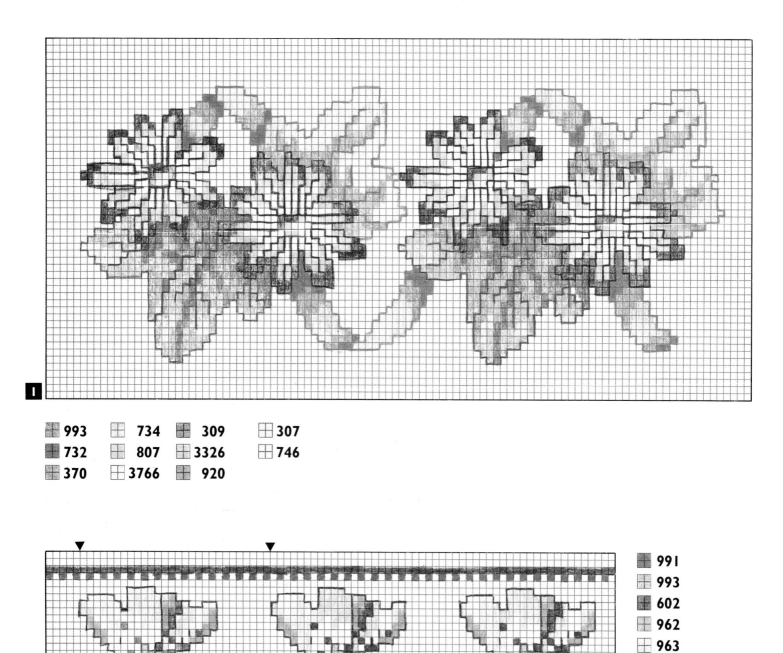

1

▦ 993	⊞ 734	▦ 309	⊞ 307
▦ 732	▦ 807	⊞ 3326	⊞ 746
▦ 370	⊞ 3766	▦ 920	

2

▦ 991
⊞ 993
▦ 602
⊞ 962
⊞ 963

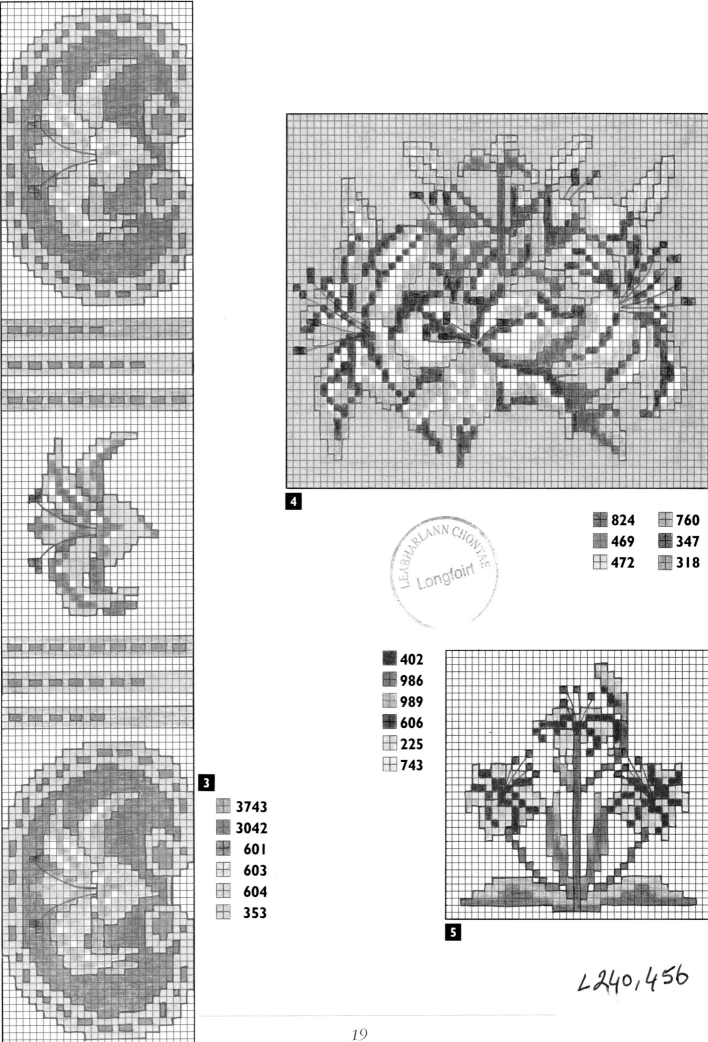

4

▦ 824	▦ 760
▦ 469	▦ 347
▦ 472	▦ 318

3

▦ 3743
▦ 3042
▦ 601
▦ 603
▦ 604
▦ 353

▦ 402
▦ 986
▦ 989
▦ 606
▦ 225
▦ 743

5

19

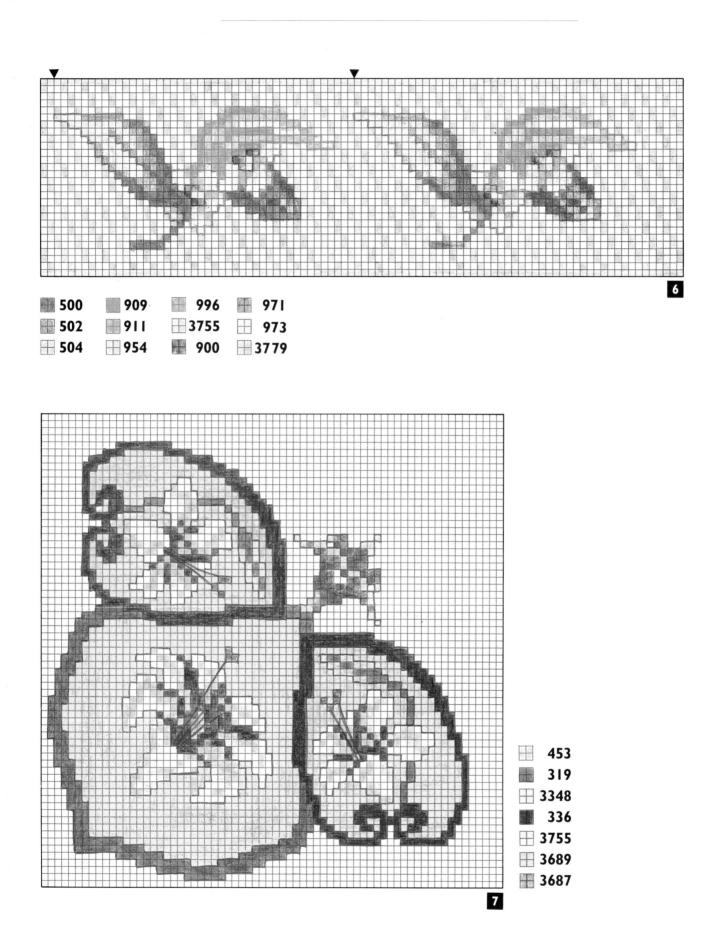

6

■ 500	■ 909	▦ 996	▦ 971
▦ 502	▦ 911	▦ 3755	▦ 973
▦ 504	▦ 954	▦ 900	▦ 3779

▦	453
■	319
▦	3348
■	336
▦	3755
▦	3689
▦	3687

7

8

⊞	**778**	⊞	**827**	⊞	**907**
⊞	**3687**	⊞	**824**	⊞	**986**
⊞	**453**				

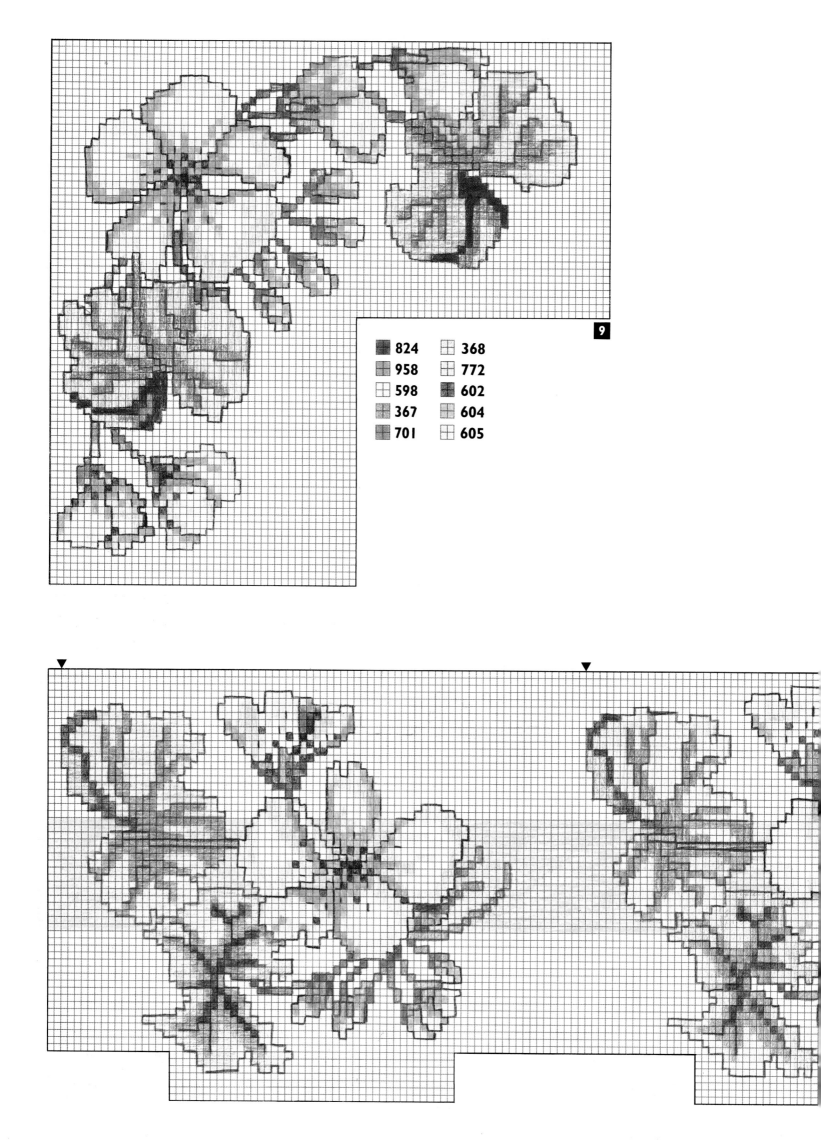

9

■ 824	⊞ 368
■ 958	⊞ 772
⊞ 598	■ 602
▦ 367	▨ 604
▦ 701	⊞ 605

⊞	3689
▦	3608
▦	3607
▦	552
⊞	742
⊞	745
⊞	3766
▦	807
▦	806
▦	414
▦	413
⊞	996

11

▦	986	⊞	747
▦	563	▦	597
▦	913	▦	598
⊞	677	▦	601
⊞	743	▦	603
▦	796	⊞	605
▦	799		

10

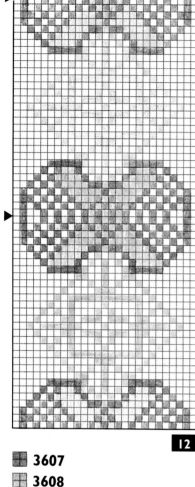

12

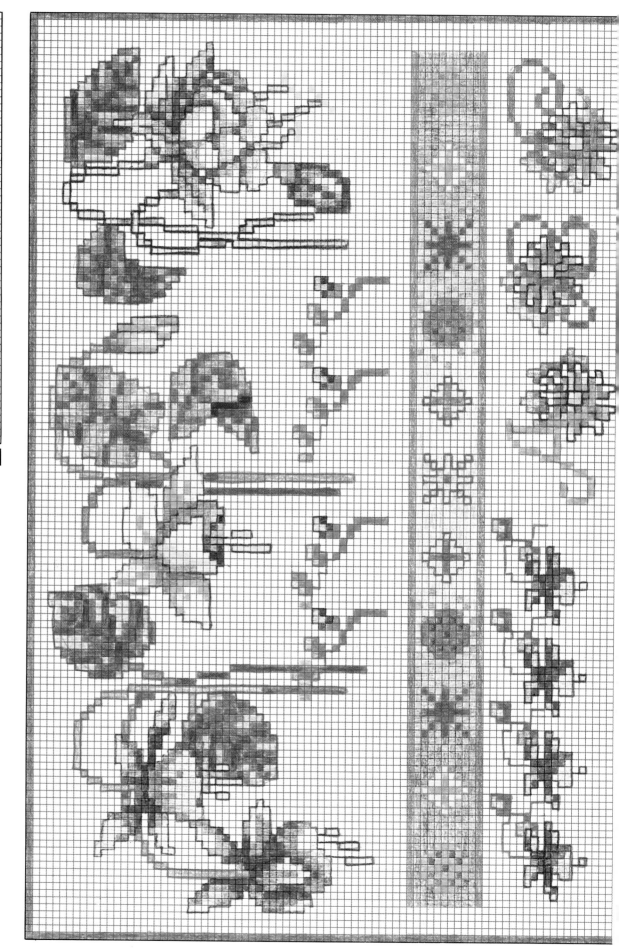

■ **3607**
▦ **3608**
▦ **3609**
▦ **945**

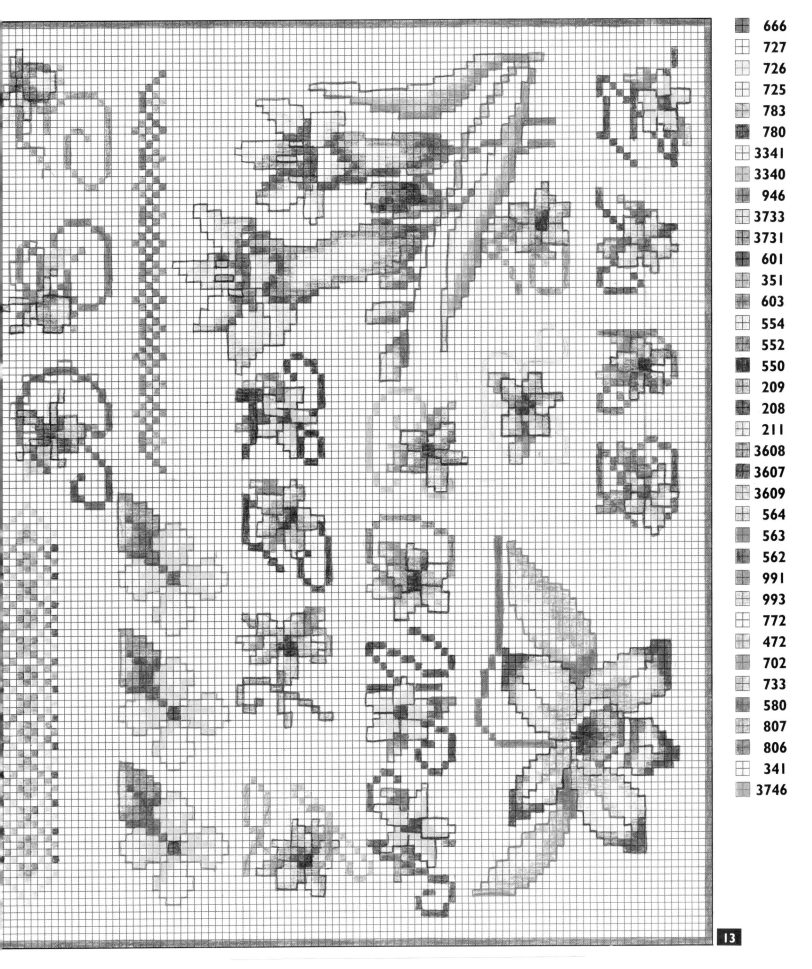

▦	666
⊞	727
⊞	726
⊞	725
▦	783
▦	780
⊞	3341
▦	3340
▦	946
▦	3733
▦	3731
▦	601
▦	351
▦	603
▦	554
▦	552
▦	550
▦	209
▦	208
⊞	211
▦	3608
▦	3607
▦	3609
⊞	564
▦	563
▦	562
▦	991
⊞	993
⊞	772
⊞	472
▦	702
⊞	733
▦	580
▦	807
▦	806
⊞	341
▦	3746

13

Inspirations in
BLUE

The sky and sea are immense blue expanses that surround us and calm our souls. Blue's diversity is seen from the light wispy colors of a foggy morning to the dark mysterious depths of the ocean. We also draw a sense of freshness, serenity, and order from this color, sometimes tinged with the haunting melancholy of the deeper tones of the musical blues.

When we wear it, blue can represent youthfulness, a sporty feeling like the universality of jeans; or, on more formal occasions, it can denote the seriousness, security, and elegance of a suit. It is even a symbol of nobility as it is said that "blue blood" flows in the veins of aristocrats.

Blue entered the world of the arts, especially the handicrafts such as mosaics, stained glass, and ceramics—where it attained unparalleled fame—from China. When the porcelain of the so-called "blue family" came to Europe, it captured the enthusiasm and the passion of many. All the large European manufacturing companies adopted blue, often making it the preferred color—the Dutch with Delft, the Danish with Royal Copenhagen, the French with Limoges, the English with Wedgwood, and the Portuguese with Azulijos. Even today, table settings and decorative items in blue tones, from the most exquisite porcelain to the most casual ceramics, have undisputed popularity.

As a result of tradition and revival trends, blue has a special place in embroidery—alongside white, blue takes on a special lightness; combined with gold, it assumes an exceptional preciousness. In both country and city homes you'll find a fresh, eternal vitality in the blue motifs featured against the whiteness of cotton and linen.

On page 27: A true classic based on ceramic pieces with a motif reproduced at regular intervals. This repetition makes it possible to lengthen or shorten the design as desired. The beautiful mirror image of the corners creates a pleasing symmetry. You can frame an entire tablecloth, or simply decorate down one side or along the bottom edge of a curtain. For maximum stylish effect, embroider the bottom of the border in cross stitch, an easy task because the lines fill up quickly and effortlessly.

Left: This sampler is a return to tradition. The many tones of blue accentuate the splendor of an impeccable piece of workmanship. The crosses create areas of shade and light, and the sampler is suggestive of an extraordinary wall panel, a picture that needs no frame. (See pp. 44–45.)

Above: This border motif is repeated to frame a group of four little blue swallows. This design makes use of just a few color tones and develops in a linear fashion with the motif pattern repeated on the same line. If the frame seems too narrow, try doubling it, repeating the mirror image on the outside. (See pp. 36 and 40.)

𝓛eft: This traditional floret runner creates a multipurpose border, perfect for a frame, on the edge of a sheet, or on lots of colored cushions to complement an all-white bed. This pattern also creates an impression of depth. First embroider the flowers and then, with perfect regularity, work the background. The final result will be richer, more defined, and very stylish if delicate contrasting tones such as rose and blue are chosen. (See p. 20.)

𝓐bove: Just as sideboard cupboards are increasing in popularity, so too are antique border patterns. They can be changed from shelf to shelf to highlight colors and classic designs such as blue porcelain. Here is a little secret on how to check what the border motif will look like as a corner: place a mirror on the diagonal of the motif so that it reflects the motif image. The combination of the motif and the reflected image will indicate the corner possibilities of the design.

*L*eft: This piece has the appearance of a tray made of fine blue porcelain. It is a wonderful design for a beautiful centerpiece to complement your accessories. Measure the size of your favorite tray—perhaps the one used each morning for breakfast—to gauge the size you will need to make the finished embroidery. It will be an elegant and cultured way to begin the day. (See pp. 46–47.)

*A*bove: The stylish little center flower from the "tray" in the opposite photo can be lifted to create a charming little bag. On a blue-gray background dotted with white, the motif has the appearance of a large, rich medallion. The plotted Aida border with a white base is folded in two and is reminiscent of the fresh decor of the twenties. Remember: on 18-count Aida, the flower will be approximately $1^{1}/_{2} \times 2^{1}/_{2}$ in. On 11-count Aida, it will be about $3 \times 3 \ ^{1}/_{2}$ in.

*O*pposite: The peony on its own can decorate a chair or a footstool to achieve a striking effect. The single flower without leaves requires 76 × 78 stitches. On 11-count Aida, the flower will measure approximately $6\frac{1}{2}$ × 7 in. It is most important, for a good result, to center the design on the fabric. Mark the center of the chart and the center of the fabric. Begin to embroider from the center.

*A*bove: The large flower, shaded in the softest tones, is a gentle peony that begs to be swirled in blue to resemble the color of clouds. For an exceptional tablecloth, one flower in each corner of the cloth is sufficient. The woven effect is obtained by working small stripes at regular intervals on the drop of the cloth. A variation would be to embroider two flowers in the center and then complete the rest of the table square in the woven design.

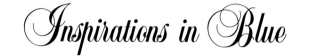

THE DESIGNS

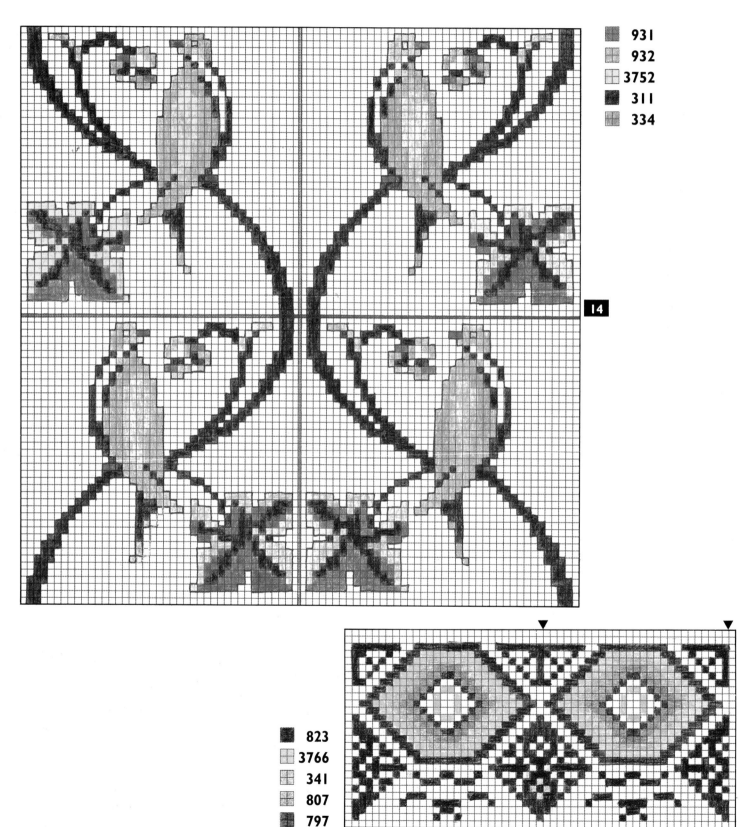

▨	931
▨	932
▨	3752
▨	311
▨	334

14

▨	823
▨	3766
▨	341
▨	807
▨	797

15

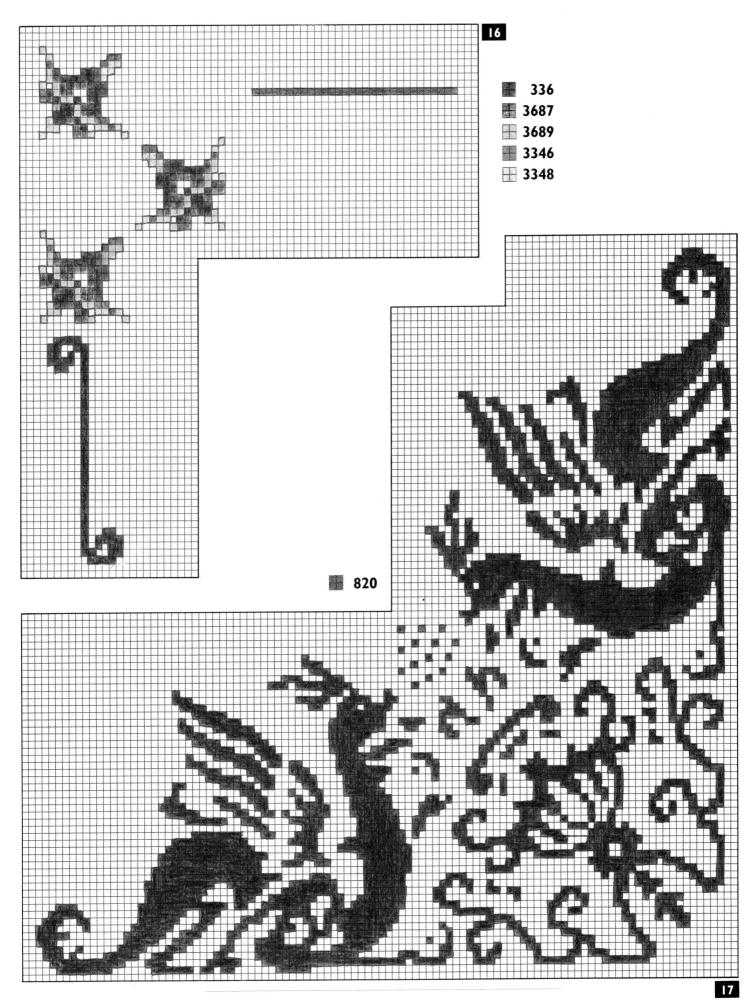

336
3687
3689
3346
3348

820

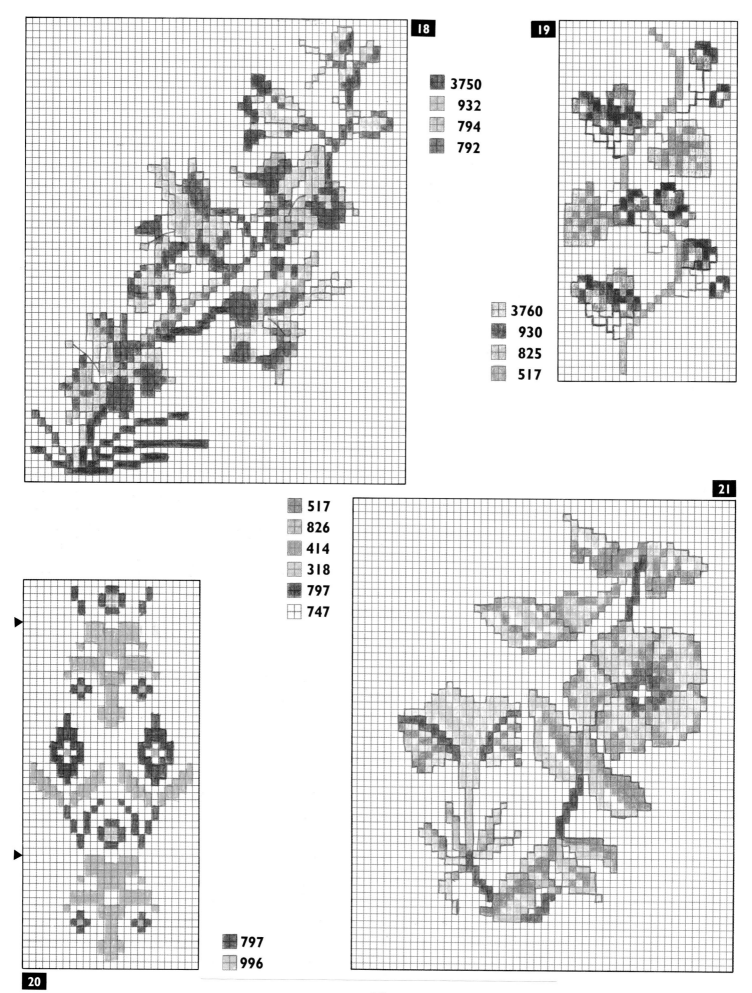

18

3750
932
794
792

19

3760
930
825
517

517
826
414
318
797
747

21

797
996

20

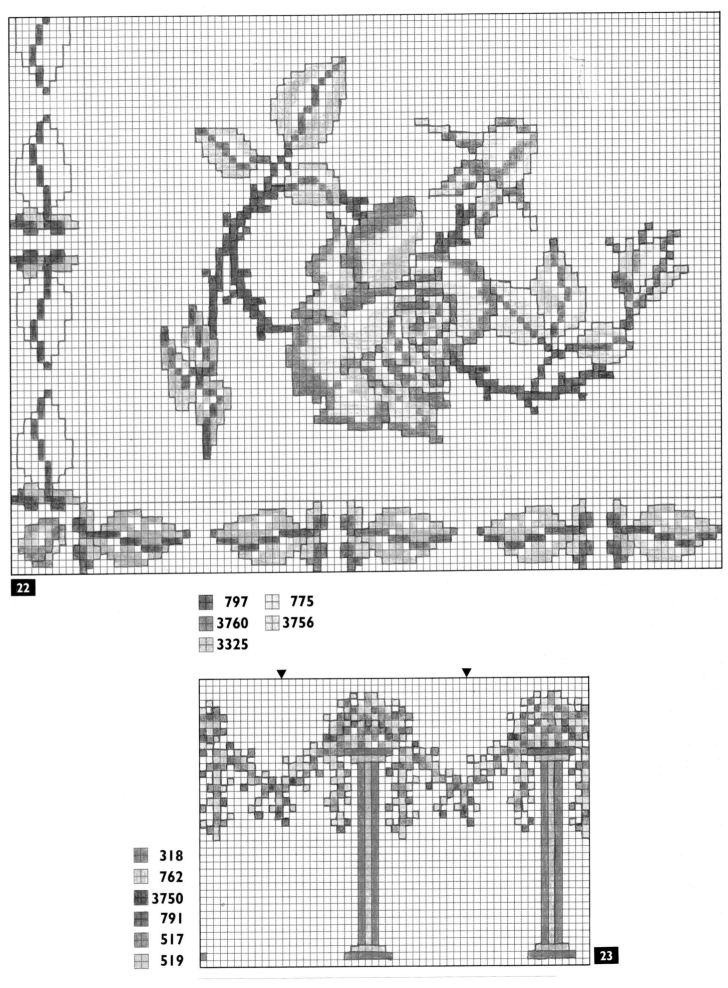

22

■ **797**	⊞ **775**
■ **3760**	⊞ **3756**
⊞ **3325**	

■	**318**
▨	**762**
■	**3750**
■	**791**
▨	**517**
▨	**519**

23

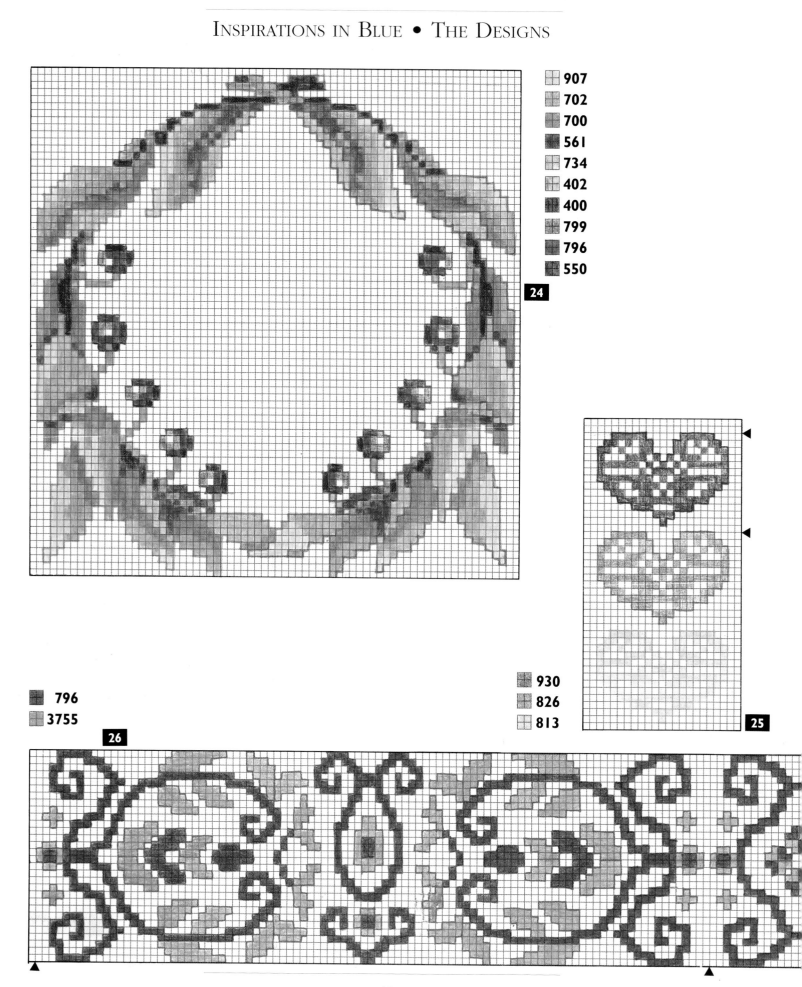

907
702
700
561
734
402
400
799
796
550

24

930
826
813

25

796
3755

26

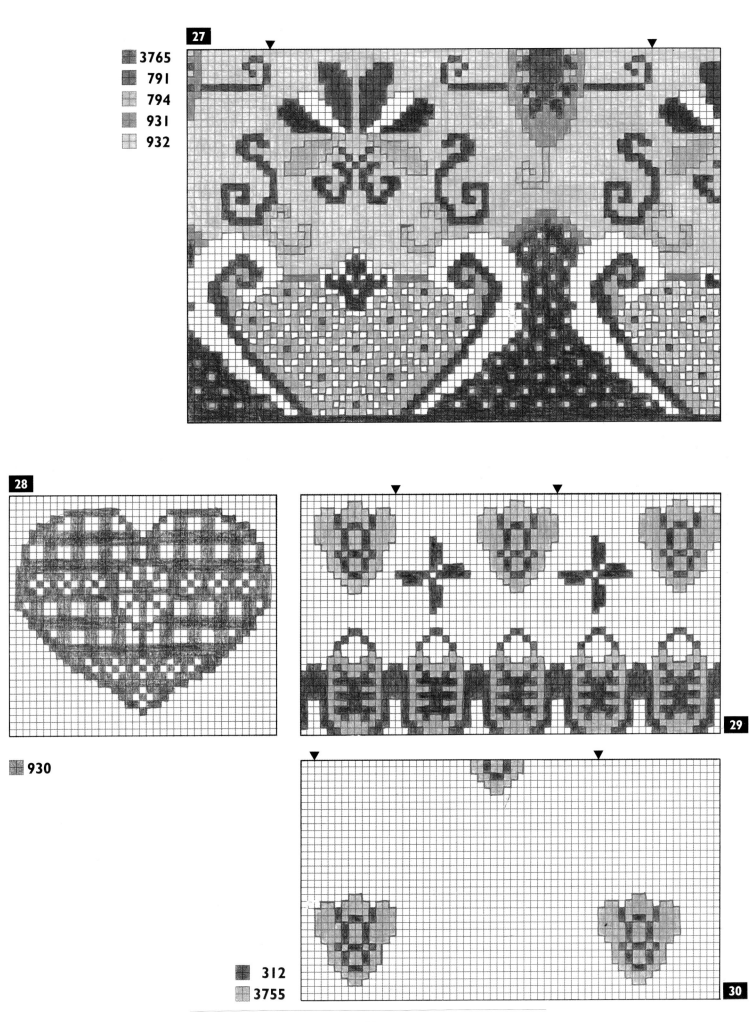

27

3765
791
794
931
932

28

29

930

30

312
3755

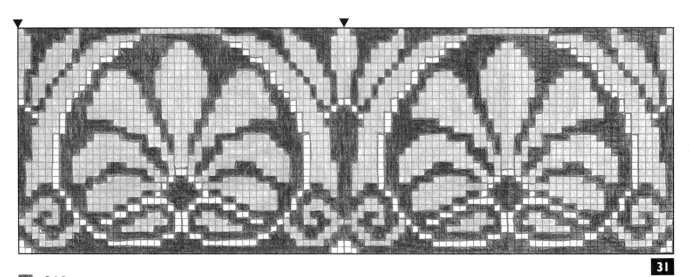

 312
3753

31

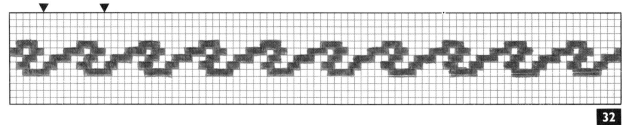

32

823

813
824

33

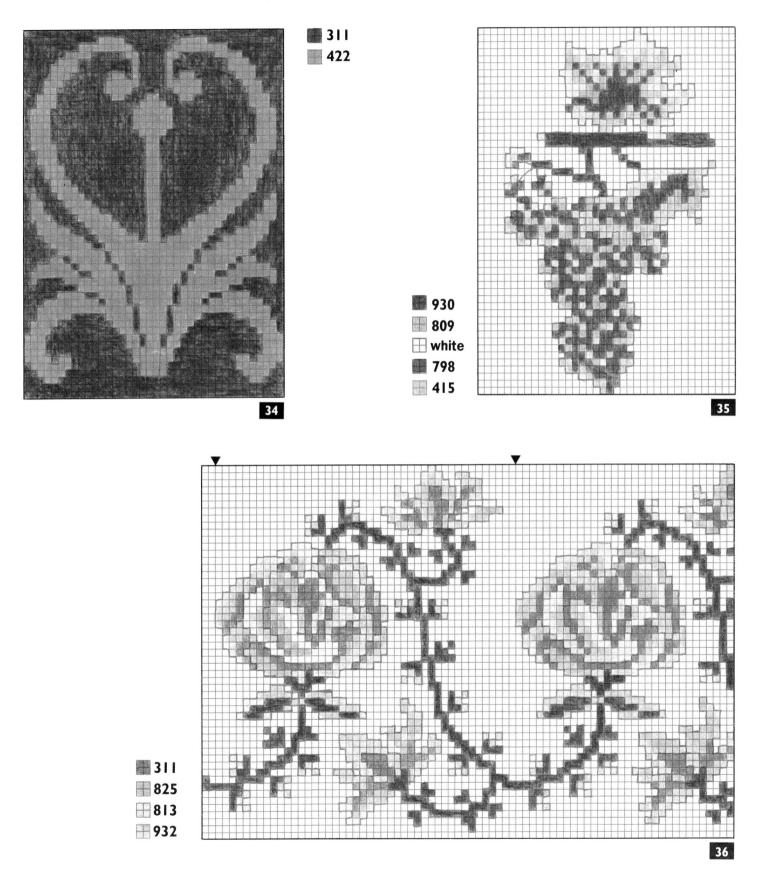

311
422

930
809
white
798
415

34

35

311
825
813
932

36

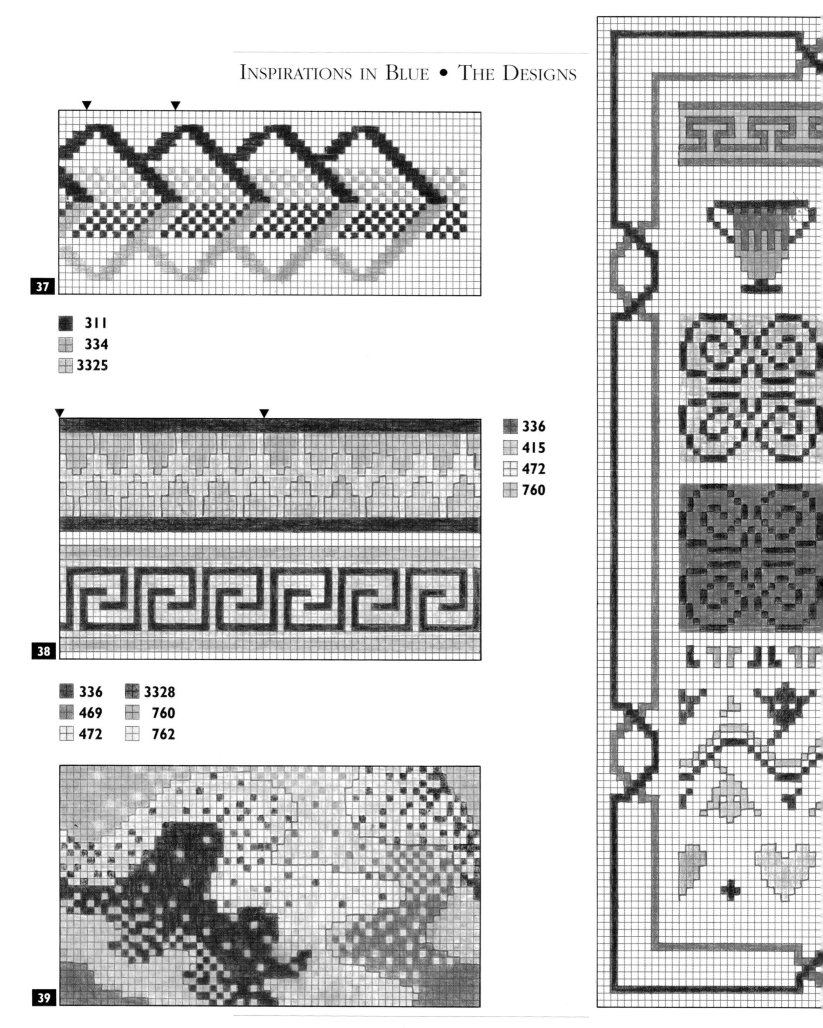

37

■ 311
▨ 334
▦ 3325

38

■ 336
▨ 415
▦ 472
▦ 760

■ 336   ▦ 3328
■ 469   ▦ 760
▦ 472   ▦ 762

39

■	798
■	3765
■	807
■	824
■	826
■	762
■	414

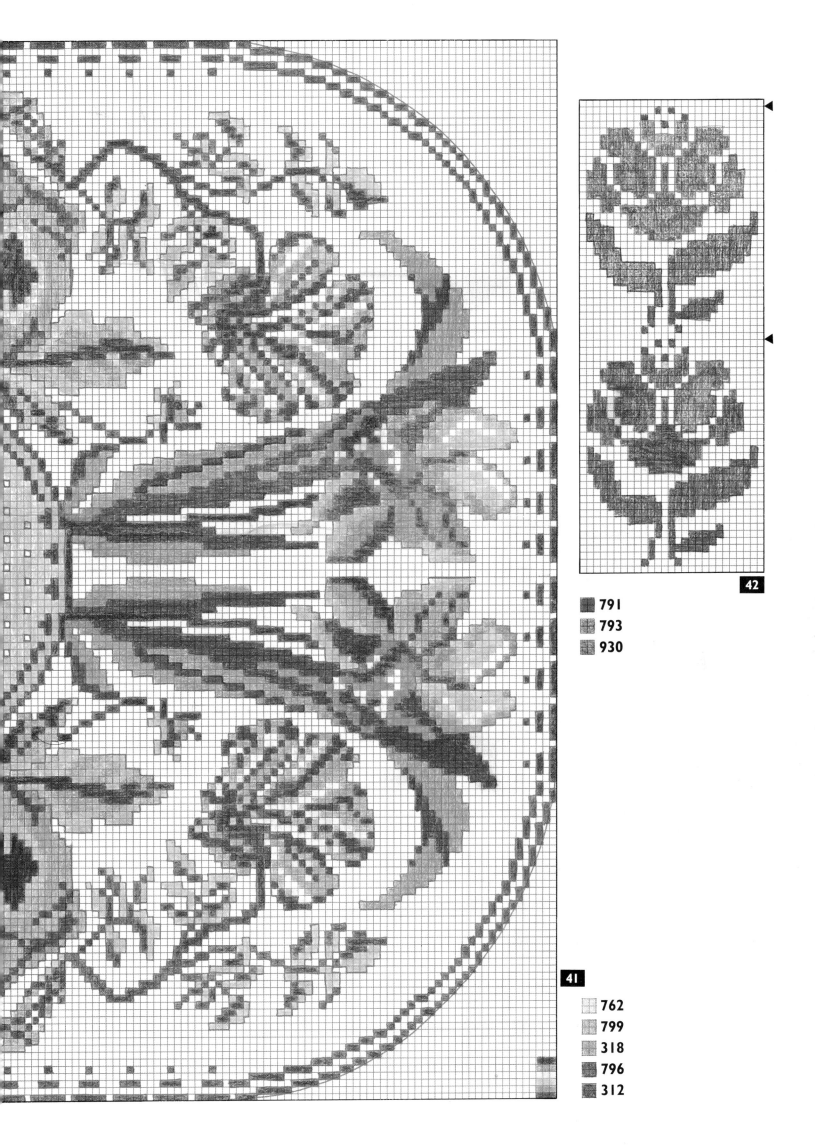

42

41

■ 791
▨ 793
▨ 930

▨ 762
▨ 799
▨ 318
■ 796
■ 312

Inspirations in
VIOLET

The blend of red and blue—opposites that attract—gives life to the most tender lilac shades and the more striking purples.

Psychologists suggest that violet represents the inner self, spirituality, and depth of feeling. According to religious tradition, it represents strength, mystery, and passion. It is a color of sensuality, power, pomp, and luxury, and was the most renowned and valued color in the Old World. We will never know what that original color's shading was, whether redder or bluer, because the murex, the mollusk from which the color was first extracted, is extinct.

With the advent of synthetic dyes, all the shades of violet once again took center stage. The French launched it into the fashion world calling it mauve, and it did especially well in Victorian England. The color violet was instrumental in bringing about another dye, called fuchsia after the flower, a particularly vibrant cross between red and blue. A few days prior to the official launch, it was renamed magenta after the battle won by the French and the Piedmonts in 1859 against the Austrians.

The natural world is full of violet—in the mineral domain, amethyst sparkles in deep violet tones; in the floral domain, violet colors various flowers: wisteria, lavender, lilac, common mallow, fuchsia, pansy, iris, and, of course, violet. This striking color blooms readily in gardens, picturesque and artistic—van Gogh painted dazzling scenes using violet.

The full cluster of our designs extol the sensuous vitality that makes violet both modern and captivating around the home.

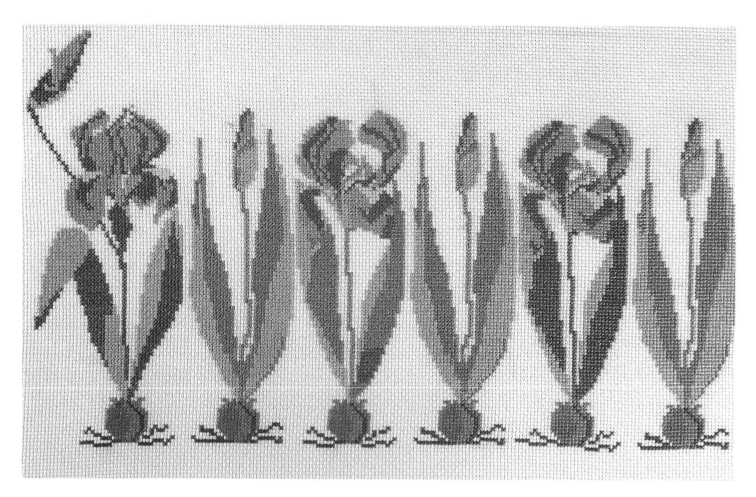

*P*age 49: This garden corner is a copy of the real thing with the art of the painter reflected in the style of the embroidery. The fascinating shades of violet, backed up by the green of the leaves and the golden tones of the ground, brilliantly capture the style of the impressionist painter. This piece would make a wonderful wall panel, cushion, bag, or screen. For a more delicate touch, use a lighter fabric; for a more striking tone, use a thicker fabric. On 18-count Aida, a single thread of floss is needed. On 14-count, use two threads.

*A*bove: From the bulbs spring narrow buds, big leaves, and bursting corollas. The incredible velvety color of the real flowers on the right is mirrored in the tone of both the painted and embroidered ones: as a runner or tablecloth, this makes a great coordinating item to give your decor both originality and cheerfulness.

*O*pposite: The motif of the iris is presented in a double row to give an outdoor look to a table runner or the band on a tablecloth; or, you can isolate a bud, as we have, for a matching touch on a napkin. You will need to precisely measure the length of the fabric against the pattern to ensure that the finished embroidery is centered. This method of repeating a motif is adopted more and more frequently because it allows greater flexibility in the use of the design.

This delightful iris motif creates a striking border with the help of an Aida fabric band. The band can be obtained in a ready-to-use form and can be attached to sheets, tablecloths, or towels. The design is adapted to fit the band. Notice in the detailed shot that space has been left above and below the band. This is to allow room for attaching the band to the selected item.

Inspirations in Violet

THE DESIGNS

	3746
	3607
	550

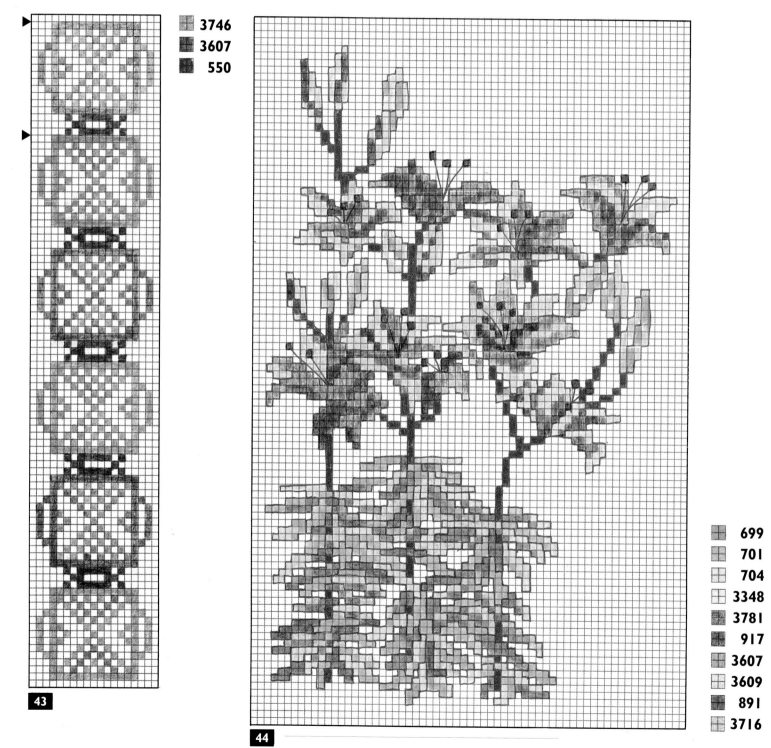

43

44

	699
	701
	704
	3348
	3781
	917
	3607
	3609
	891
	3716

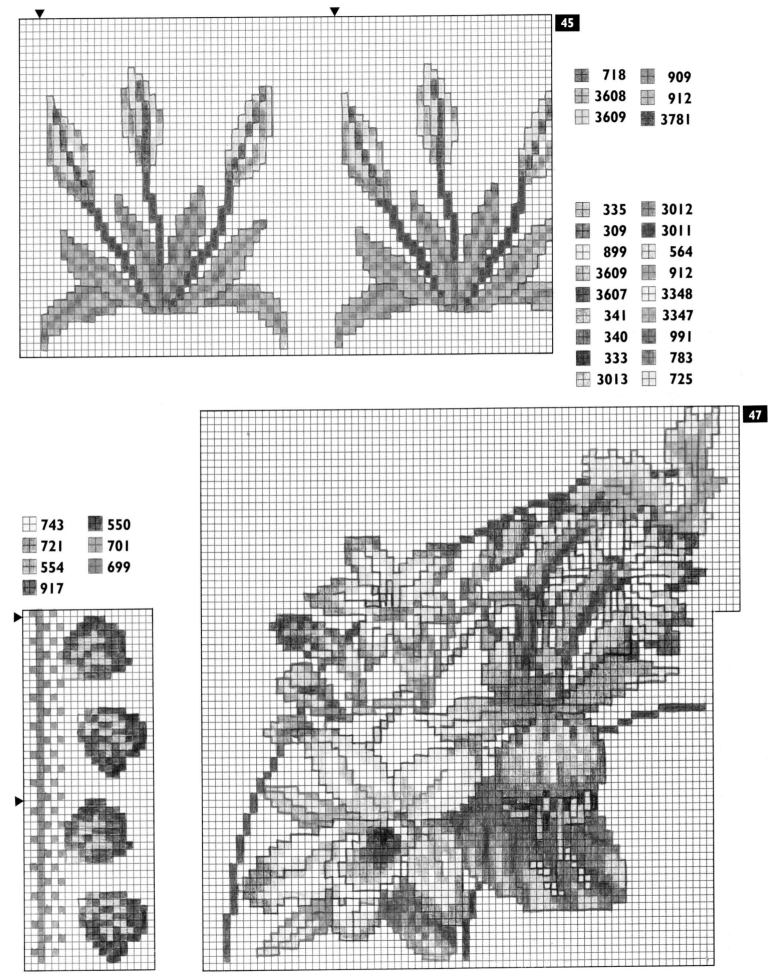

45

▦	718	▦	909
▦	3608	▦	912
▦	3609	▦	3781

▦	335	▦	3012
▦	309	▦	3011
▦	899	▦	564
▦	3609	▦	912
▦	3607	▦	3348
▦	341	▦	3347
▦	340	▦	991
▦	333	▦	783
▦	3013	▦	725

47

▦	743	▦	550
▦	721	▦	701
▦	554	▦	699
▦	917		

46

55

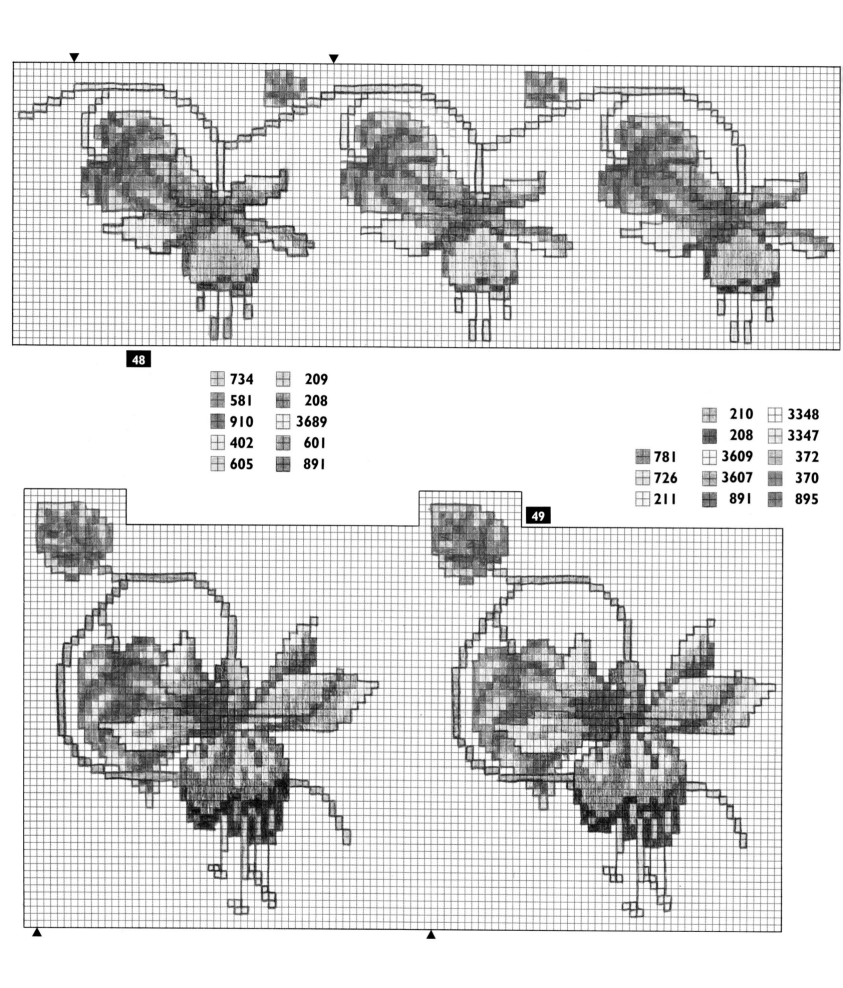

48

⊞ 734	⊞ 209		
▦ 581	⊞ 208		
▦ 910	⊞ 3689		
⊞ 402	▦ 601		
⊞ 605	▦ 891		

		⊞ 210	⊞ 3348
		▦ 208	⊞ 3347
▦ 781	⊞ 3609		▦ 372
⊞ 726	⊞ 3607		▦ 370
⊞ 211	▦ 891		▦ 895

49

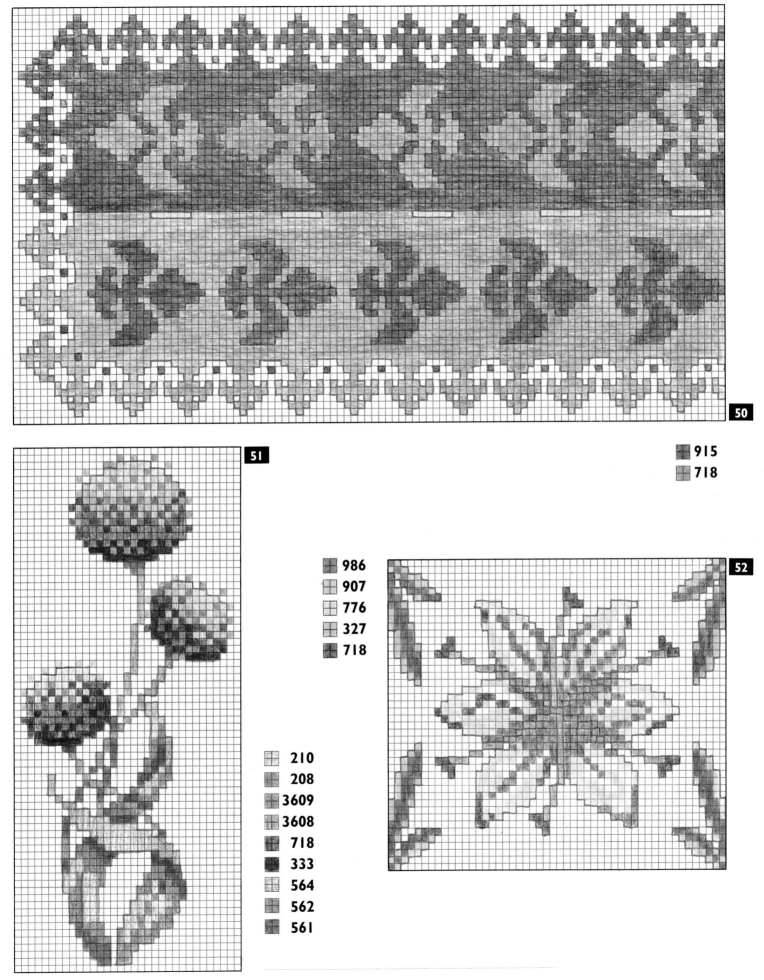

50

915
718

51

986
907
776
327
718

210
208
3609
3608
718
333
564
562
561

52

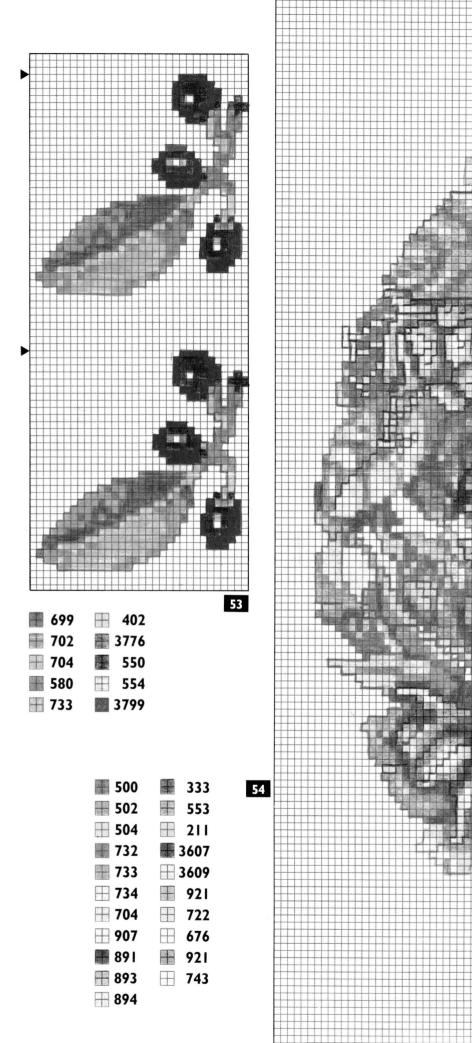

53

	699		402
	702		3776
	704		550
	580		554
	733		3799

54

	500		333
	502		553
	504		211
	732		3607
	733		3609
	734		921
	704		722
	907		676
	891		921
	893		743
	894		

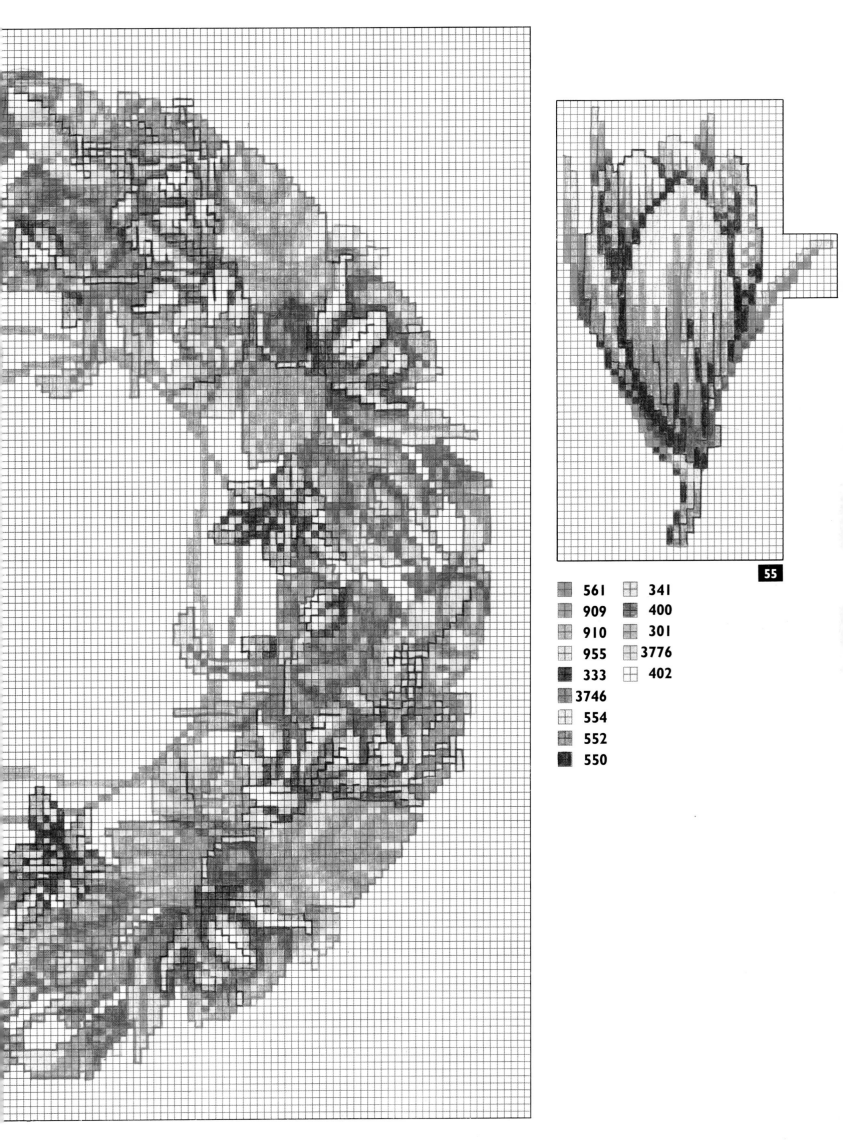

561   341
909   400
910   301
955   3776
333
3746
554
552
550

55

Inspirations in

YELLOW

$\mathcal{L}$et yourself be inspired and captivated by the brilliance of yellow—a beautiful color that is full of sunshine. It looks wonderful on a table, and the color radiates from flowers like mimosas and jonquils. Yellow captures attention like the tang of lemon or grapefruit. It harmonizes beautifully with wood and takes on an old gold glow. In the Far East, it was the color of the emperor. To Buddhists it represents the harmony of existence. It is the color of light and as such it is joyful and triumphant.

It has brilliant clarity that can be shaded towards ochre, brown, or green. It abounds in nature: saffron and banana, egg yolk and ripe wheat, buttercups and sunflowers, canary feathers and cat's-eyes. It is also the color of gold—symbol of the earth's riches and the highest sign of glory, power, and triumph.

In springtime, gardens flourish with the yellow hues of daffodils, crocus, primroses, and freesias. Even tender new leaves have traces of yellow within their green. And, in the kitchen, it is a most appealing color—the one that evokes savory associations with the bounty of the table and the pleasure of food. Yellow is a wonderful color to embroider, working in sunshine and cheerfulness, gathering life stitch by stitch.

$\mathcal{P}$ages 60–61: The light
of yellow glows against the
white Aida as it forms a
zigzag of narcissus. This
effect is sunny and cheerful
when the design is worked
along the drop of a
tablecloth, on the side of a
sampler, on a sheet, on a
small curtain, on a
pinafore—or, in fact,
anywhere. It is even
possible to work out a
corner design, using the
mirror on the diagonal, or
stopping the embroidery at
the last flower and taking it
up again on the other side.
With corners you need only
a small connecting motif
such as a rhombus or a
small star. (See p. 68.)

$\mathcal{L}$eft and above: The
ribbon and flower shoots
create a playful and
enchanting tablecloth. The
ribbon wraps itself around
a fine sequence of juniper
berries in aerial spirals rich
in careful shading. The
pattern can also be
repeated on the drop of the
cloth. For decoration along
the sides, try splitting the
two motif shoots and
alternating them in a
balanced fashion within the
empty spaces. Remember
to mark the spots for the
motifs at the beginning by
basting to achieve even
spacing. (See p. 69.)

*A*bove: A close-up section of the very fresh looking sampler on the right that allows us to see and fully appreciate the shadings and tones. It also enables the easy counting of the cross stitches to accurately re-create a clear graph for a perfect result.

*R*ight: The full flavor of summer with baskets full of peaches and ripe pears, letters intertwined with juniper berries, and colored bonsai. This sampler could be framed as a decoration for a wall, or the individual elements could be lifted out to become motifs for larger works. Begin the embroidery at the top left-hand corner and proceed diagonally toward the bottom right. (See pp. 72–73.)

*L*eft: Fruit is featured once more in rows and groups and in wicker baskets: grapes, figs, oranges, bananas, and cherries. All appear more lifelike due to the rich shading. This design can be used as a panel for the pages of a calendar or a weekly planner for meals. This planner would be perfect hanging in the kitchen mounted on a rectangular plywood frame that could even be lightly padded.

*T*his page: A closer look at the woven baskets shows how each one is different from the other. Each basket also holds different fruits in natural colors. The fruit baskets can be copied without difficulty and reproduced in the center of a tablecloth or at the bottom of a curtain. They will provide a cheerful accent.

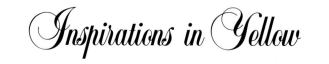

THE DESIGNS

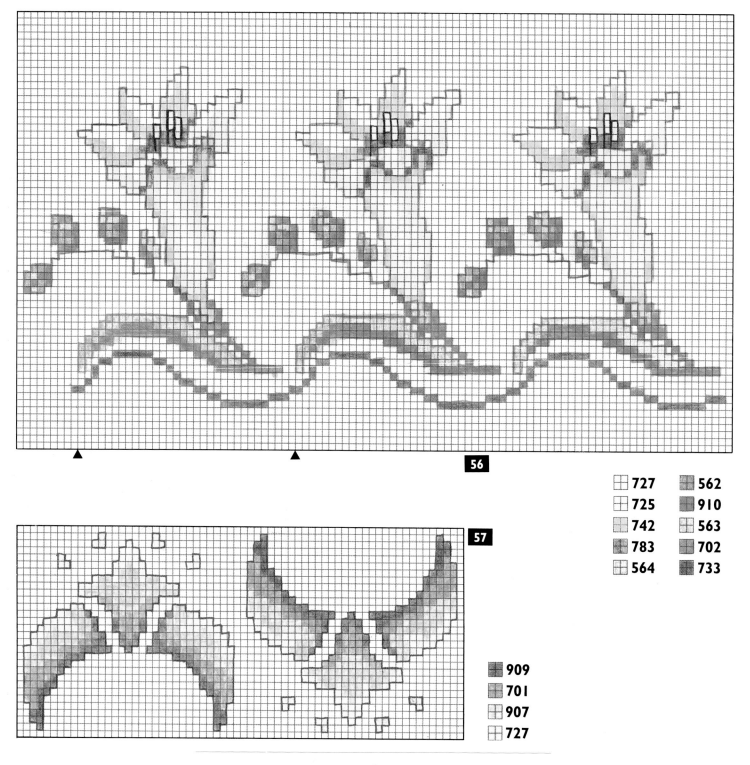

⊞ 727	▦ 562
⊞ 725	▦ 910
⊞ 742	⊞ 563
▦ 783	▦ 702
⊞ 564	▦ 733

56

57

▦ 909
▦ 701
⊞ 907
⊞ 727

68

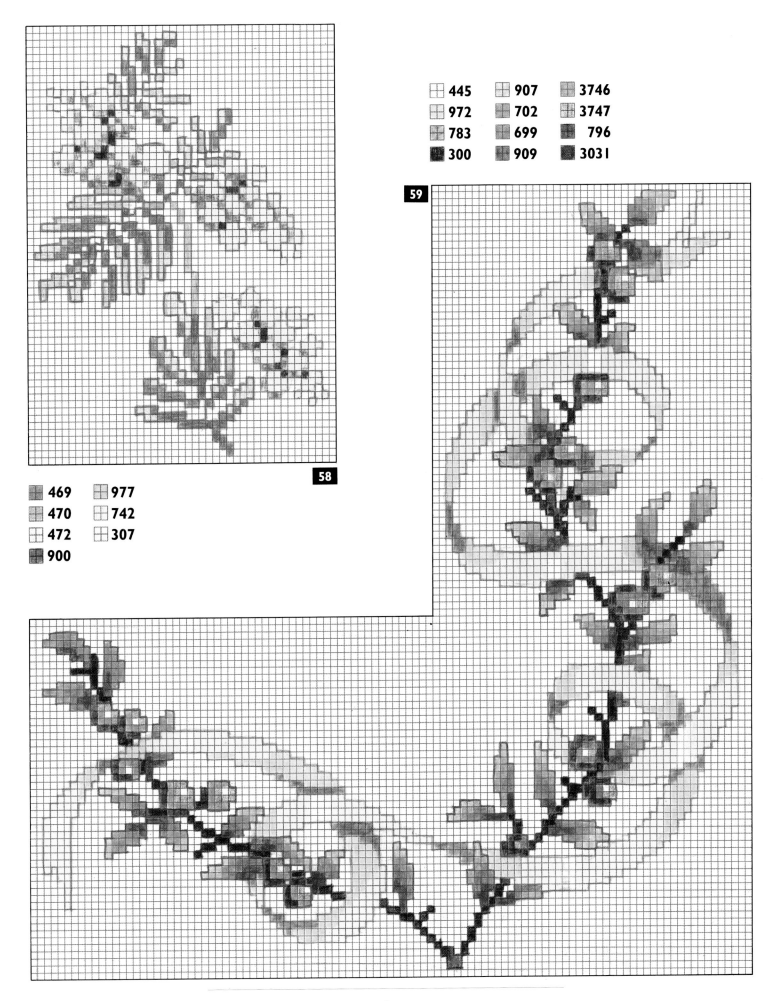

445   907   3746
972   702   3747
783   699   796
300   909   3031

59

58

469   977
470   742
472   307
900

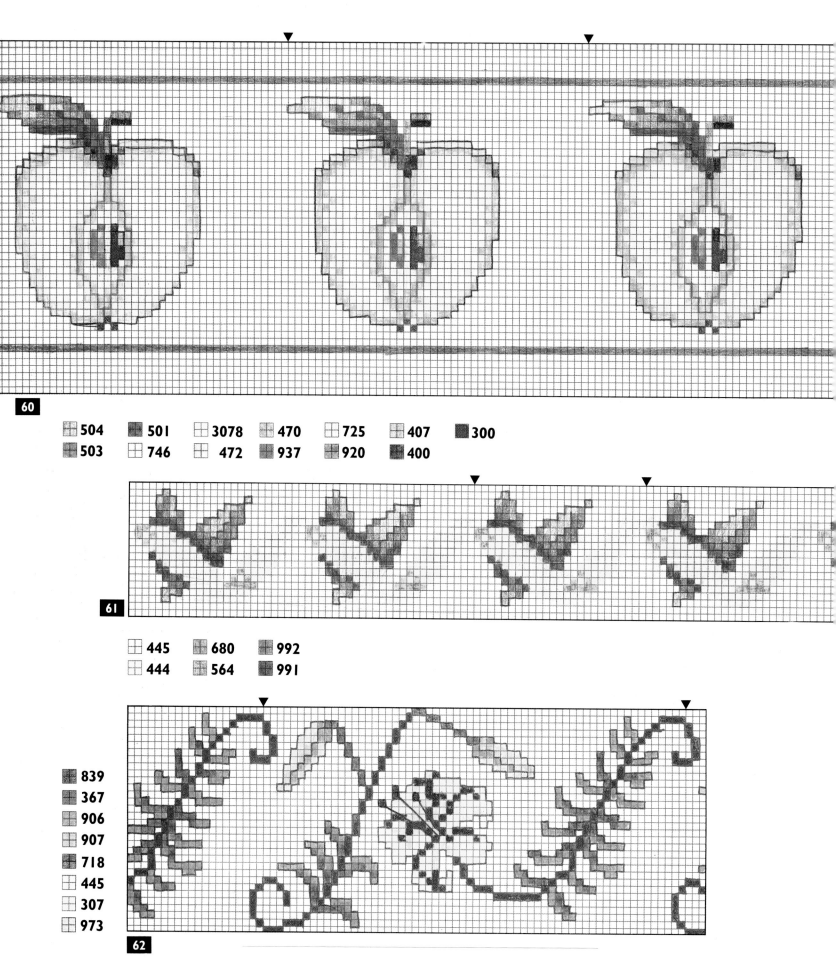

60

⊞ 504	■ 501	⊞ 3078	⊞ 470	⊞ 725	⊞ 407	■ 300
⊞ 503	⊞ 746	⊞ 472	■ 937	⊞ 920	■ 400	

61

⊞ 445	⊞ 680	■ 992
⊞ 444	⊞ 564	■ 991

■ 839
■ 367
■ 906
⊞ 907
■ 718
⊞ 445
⊞ 307
⊞ 973

62

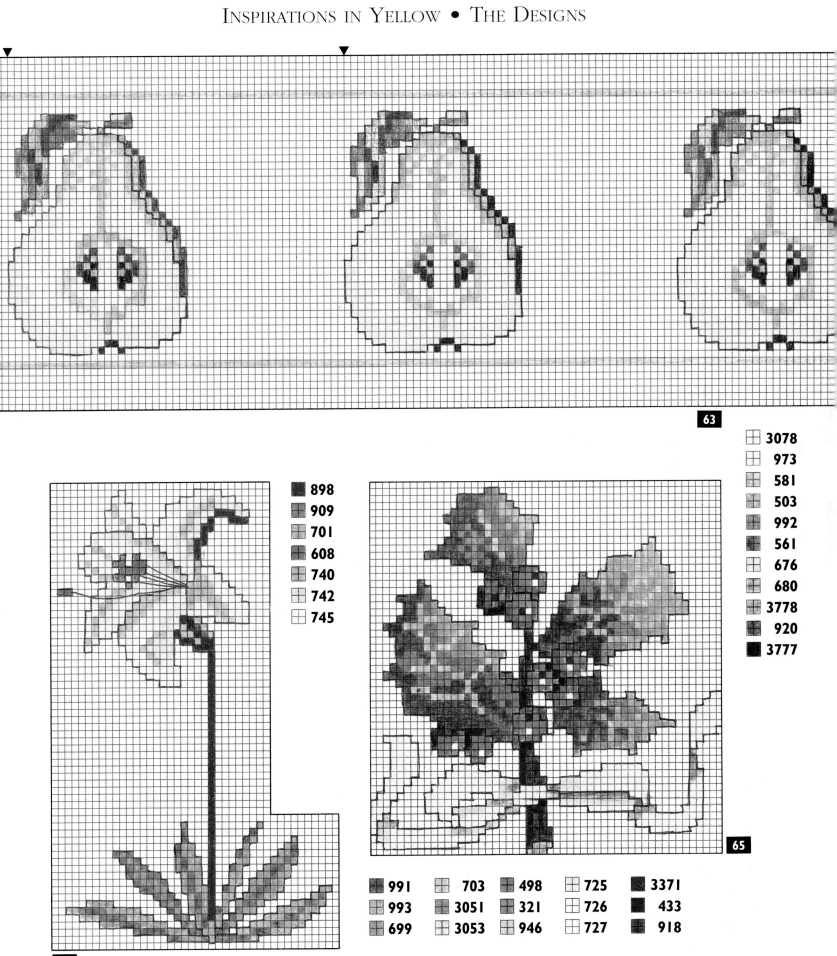

63

⊞	**3078**		
⊞	**973**		
⊞	**581**		
⊞	**503**		
⊞	**992**		
⊞	**561**		
⊞	**676**		
⊞	**680**		
⊞	**3778**		
⊞	**920**		
⊞	**3777**		

■	**898**
⊞	**909**
⊞	**701**
⊞	**608**
⊞	**740**
⊞	**742**
⊞	**745**

65

64

■ **991**	⊞ **703**	■ **498**	⊞ **725**	■ **3371**
⊞ **993**	⊞ **3051**	■ **321**	⊞ **726**	■ **433**
⊞ **699**	⊞ **3053**	⊞ **946**	⊞ **727**	⊞ **918**

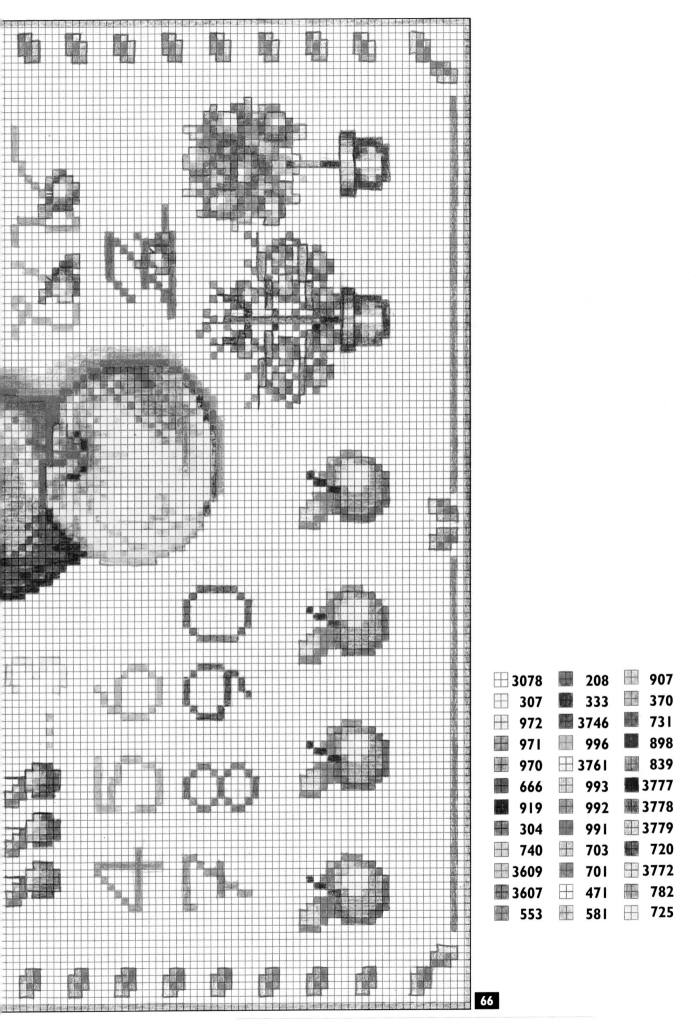

3078	208	907
307	333	370
972	3746	731
971	996	898
970	3761	839
666	993	3777
919	992	3778
304	991	3779
740	703	720
3609	701	3772
3607	471	782
553	581	725

66

Inspirations in
ORANGE

$\mathcal{C}$reated by blending red and yellow, orange dazzles in its many shades. For centuries it had no real identity of its own and had to yield to the stronger impact of red. Flames of fire or strands of auburn hair, for example, both have chromatic tones that are, strictly speaking, part of the color orange but have traditionally been defined as red. A few centuries ago, the citrus fruit, aurantium, came to Europe from the Far East. Its decisive coloring and its exquisite, succulent pulp made a strong impression, and the fruit was given the name orange.

From a psychological viewpoint, orange remains closer to yellow than red—cheerful, expansive, extroverted, and sun-filled. In the garden, autumn is orange's season, as the leaves become golden and tawny. Other fruits with orange pulp are the mango, the persimmon, and the apricot. In the vegetable domain, orange is found in the familiar carrot, squash, and pumpkin. A darker tone is found in certain exotic spices such as the intoxicating cinnamon. An earthy shade like no other, orange is found in the iron deposits that tinge many rocks, including amber, quartz, and carnelian, and in certain types of wood that are tawny rather than white.

The flames of a fireplace also reflect a brown-orange light tone that warms up surrounding terra-cotta and brick. For this reason alone, orange cannot be omitted from embroidery threads because it represents a sense of home and welcome: the warmth from the chimney, the glow from the hearth, symbolic and central to the meaning of family.

Pages 74–76: Spots of warming light with explosions of rich color tones that highlight rustic beauty in the center of a tablecloth. With a square tablecloth, the motifs should be equidistant from each other. With a rectangular cloth, the long sides should be interspersed with small clusters of fruit and leaves, which can also be featured on the drop of the tablecloth and on napkins. Thanks to cross stitch, the ribbon has all the richness of a strip of satin, and the blue flowers perfectly set off the ripening fruit. (See p. 84.)

Right: Here we have fruits of the forest surrounded by green, then finished with rich strokes of sunny tones. Only a few leaves and a simple vine shoot are needed to create a colorful splash on a tablecloth, towel, curtain, or sheet. For this design, repeating the motif is very effective and results in a rich border.

*L*eft: A branch of wood, a shoot of vine leaves, and clusters of juniper berries on this fabric kindle the desire to be surrounded by natural colors. The design unfolds in zigzag fashion on a strip measuring 70 stitches in length, and whether the branch finishes on the right or the left, the motif can be repeated as often as desired. (See p. 87.)

*A*bove: Orange hues suit this design admirably. The playful leaves lend excitement to the napkin, which is no larger than 42 stitches in length. This pattern gives the table an unusual charm. Before beginning the embroidery, carefully plan the motifs in order to explore the numerous adaptations possible with regard to the desired look of the finished piece; to decorate the corners, embroider two branches, joining them with a small sprinkling of leaves.

*L*eft: Delicious looking miniature fruits are quick to work in cross stitch. Embroidered with two threads, cross-stitch and topiary-like fruit trees make a delightfully different combination. A panel decorated with lots of little trees of the same design might create a stunning headboard. Cushions and other soft furnishings can be decorated with small trees of two different sizes. The possibilities are appealing, simple, and endless. (See p. 86.)

*A*bove: Simplicity, beauty, and color are the three best qualities of cross stitch. This basic design illustrates how a simple tablecloth can be transformed into a showpiece with the repetition of a motif along the border—the end result is a colorful latticework design. The shape of the tablecloth is not important, as the design can be spaced to suit.

THE DESIGNS

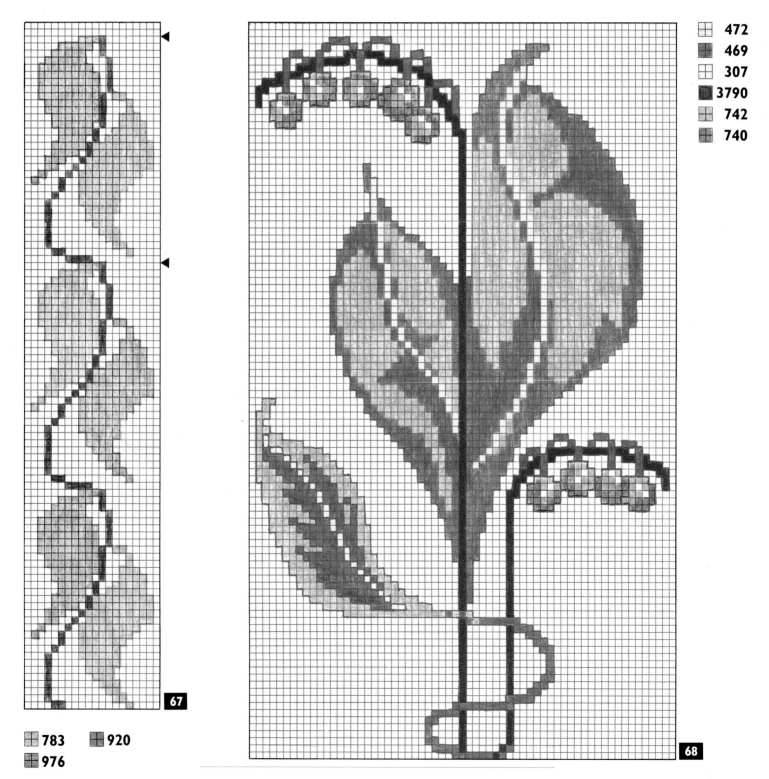

	472
	469
	307
	3790
	742
	740

67

	783		920
	976		

68

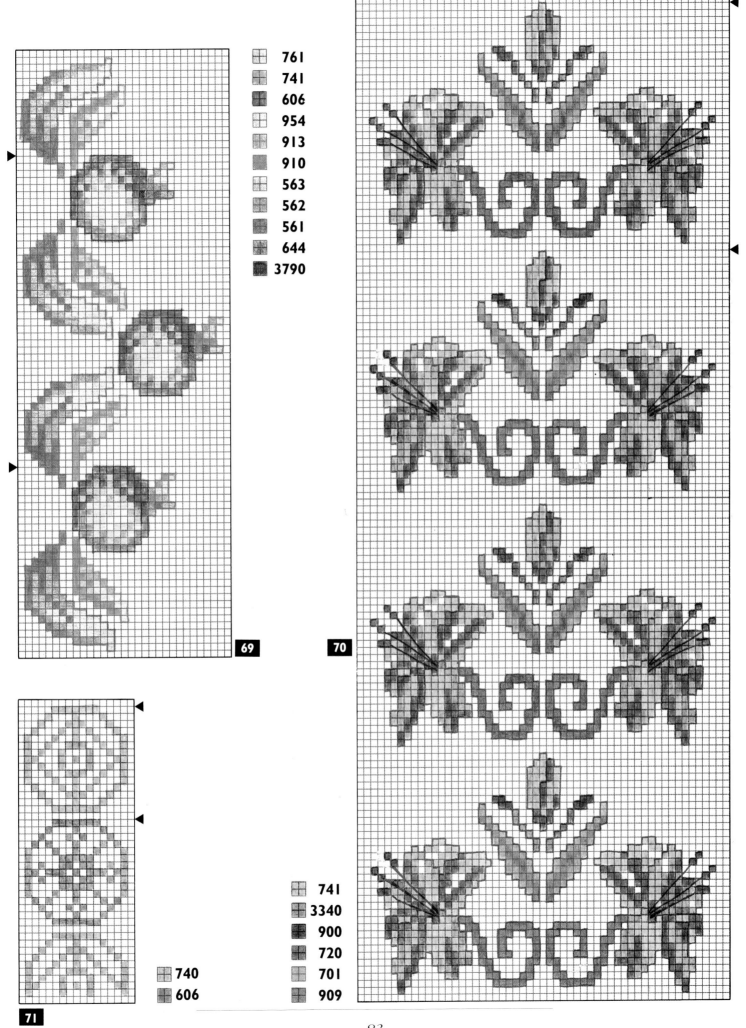

761
741
606
954
913
910
563
562
561
644
3790

69

70

71

740
606

741
3340
900
720
701
909

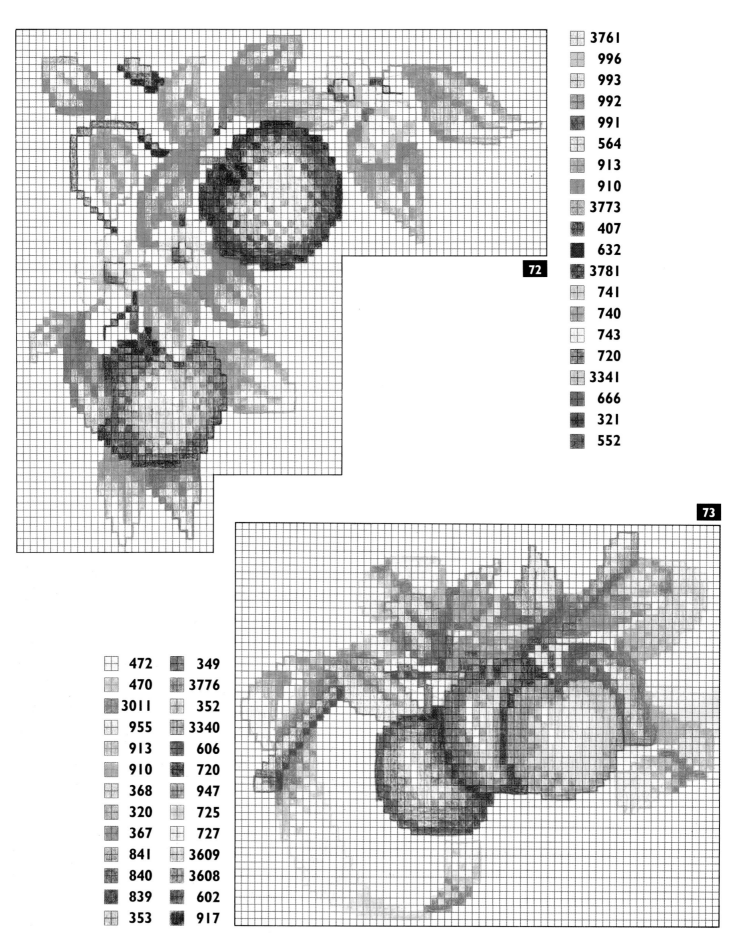

72

▦	3761
▦	996
▦	993
▦	992
▦	991
▦	564
▦	913
▦	910
▦	3773
▦	407
▦	632
▦	3781
▦	741
▦	740
▦	743
▦	720
▦	3341
▦	666
▦	321
▦	552

73

▦	472	▦	349
▦	470	▦	3776
▦	3011	▦	352
▦	955	▦	3340
▦	913	▦	606
▦	910	▦	720
▦	368	▦	947
▦	320	▦	725
▦	367	▦	727
▦	841	▦	3609
▦	840	▦	3608
▦	839	▦	602
▦	353	▦	917

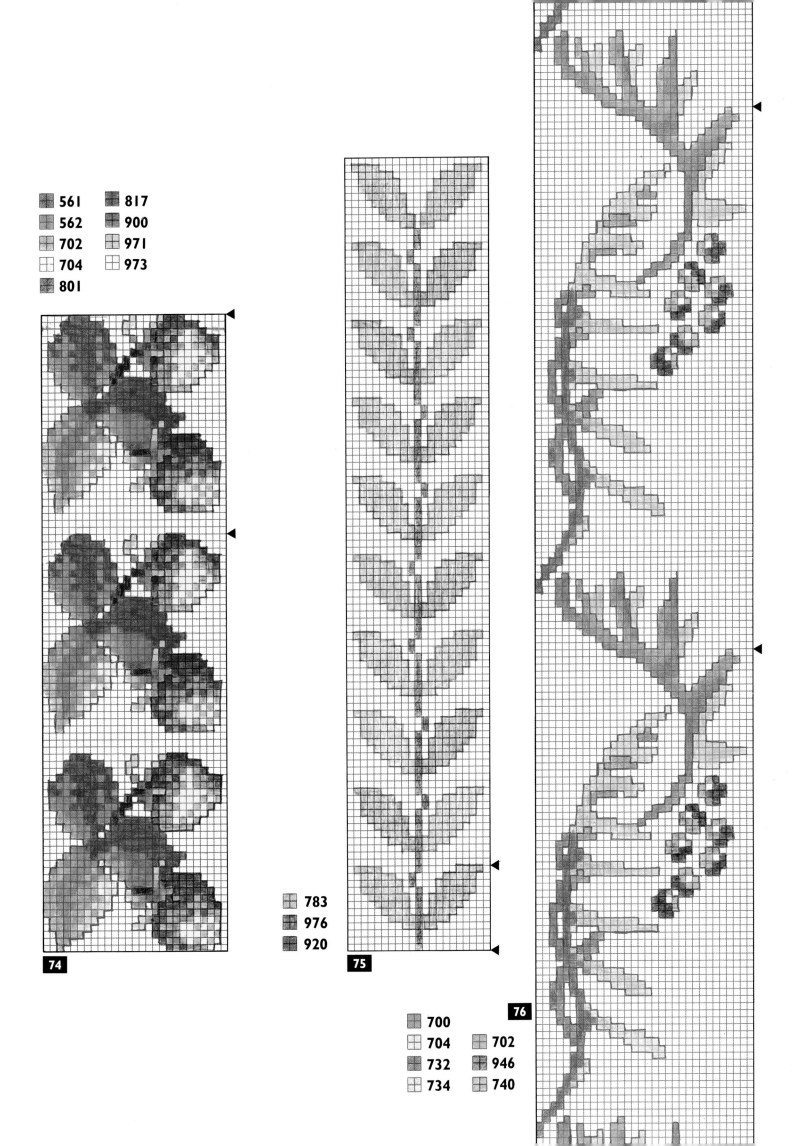

561   817
562   900
702   971
704   973
801

74

783
976
920

75

700
704   702
732   946
734   740

76

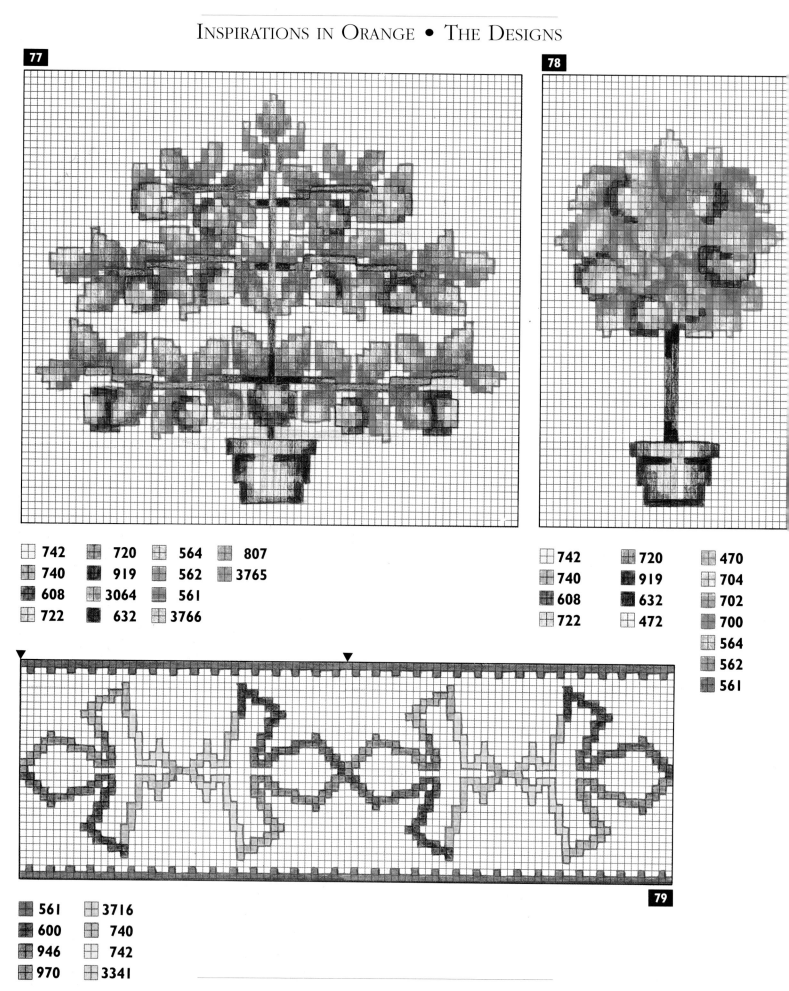

77

742		720		564		807		
740		919		562		3765		
608		3064		561				
722		632		3766				

78

742		720		470
740		919		704
608		632		702
722		472		700
				564
				562
				561

79

561		3716
600		740
946		742
970		3341

81

⊞	3341
⬛	350
⬛	817
⬛	975
⊞	977
⬛	731
⊞	472
⊞	702
⬛	700
⬛	699

80

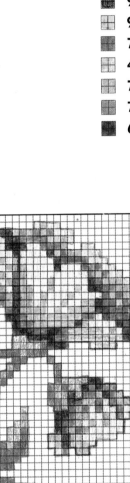

⊞	3779	⬛	919
⊞	722	⊞	504
⬛	720	⊞	502

Inspirations in
RED

*S*top! Attention! Danger! Red also indicates courage, daring, and dynamism. Red is the color of the blood that pulses in our veins, the heart that beats in our breast; it expresses the strongest of emotions, the most intense feelings and sensations. The attributes of red are nearly always superlatives. It is at the top of the rainbow. It is the first tone to strike the conscious self when we wake up. More than any other color it attracts the eye, mesmerizes, gives weight, touches the soul, and unleashes anger and rage.

Passion is red, as are the pleasures of the senses. Red is sumptuous, rich and regal, flashy, symbolic, spectacular—hence the color of the stage curtain and of the carpet we roll out to welcome dignitaries and heroes. It is the color that best expresses the joy and excitement of festivals like Christmas—the cheerfulness of the juniper berries amidst the green holly, apples amongst the spruce branches, ribbons and bows on presents under the sparkling tree. It is the sharp, tempting color of irresistible fruits—cherries, strawberries, raspberries, and red currants. It is the hot flavor of that most sublime food, the spicy red chili pepper.

In embroidery, red has always held a very secure place. In the last century it was the color used for numbers or initials sewn on personal linens. Its deep tones denote richness and its lighter tones youth and vivaciousness. Red thread has the capacity to enrich a fabric and highlight any design.

$\mathcal{P}$age 88–89: The border pattern of small cherries creates a striking effect on an old sideboard cabinet. Larger motifs would look great on a carpet. Alternatively, a single small cherry could be embroidered onto a very fine fabric such as pure linen and made into a brooch using doubled thread. (See p. 98.)

$\mathcal{L}$eft: The red of the juniper berry contrasts with the green shade of the leaves. This fresh, innocent design, never tedious or unappealing, is often used in the embroidery tradition of cross stitch. It is popular, no doubt, because of the beauty of line, the cheerful colors, and for its appeal as a decoration. A helpful hint: do a quick sketch of the design, in color and drawn to scale, to gauge an idea of the finished piece before beginning cross stitching. (See p. 96.)

$\mathcal{A}$bove: A bouquet, a ribbon, and lots of complementary colors give this piece of embroidery style and class. This design would be ideal for a cushion, a linen bag, or a handkerchief. (See p. 99.)

*A*bove and right: A wreath creates a festive season on a tablecloth, a tray, or a cushion. Take care to center the motif by planning the exact position. Count the stitches both vertically and horizontally to make a square, and trace the diagonals. Do the same on the fabric and begin embroidering on the vertical point in the center. (See pp. 100–101.)

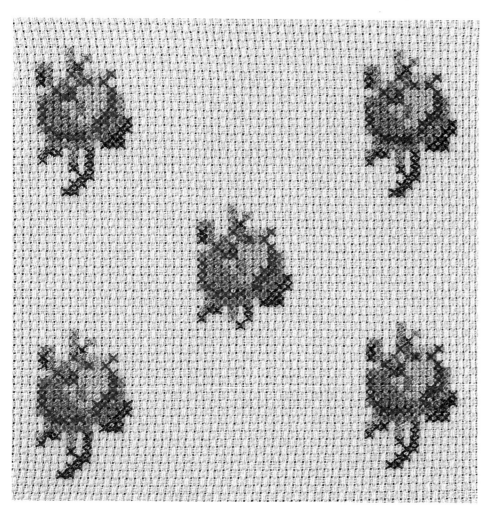

𝒜bove and right: Each unique in design, these small, graceful touches of light create a charming design for a tablecloth. Using all the different variations, the very striking effect will resemble a classical damask of fine silk from the 1800s. This wonderful piece illustrates perfectly the subtle fascination of an easy stitch that never varies its geometric repetition, yet can be transformed and enhanced with color and design.

THE DESIGNS

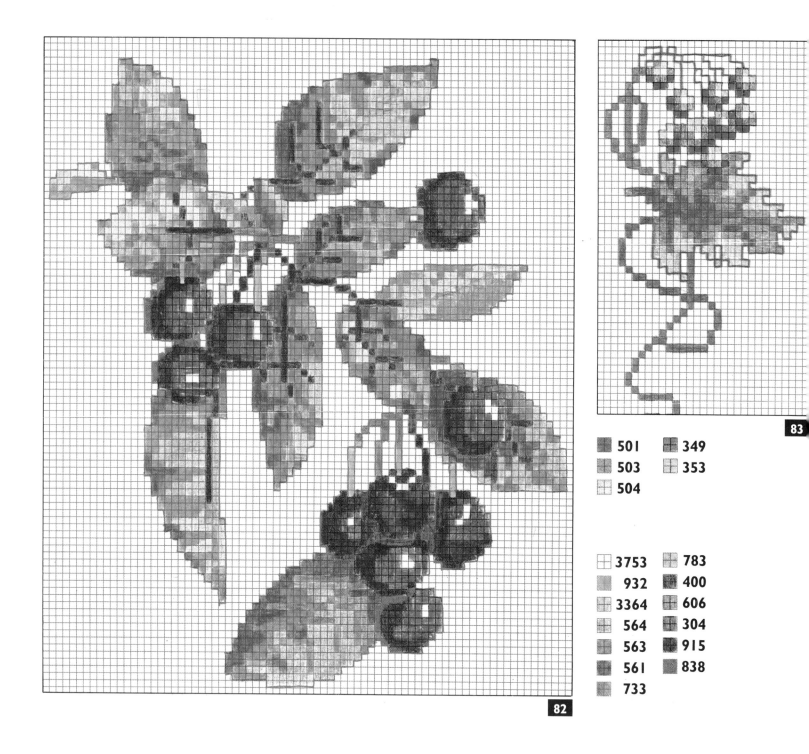

■ 501	▦ 349
▦ 503	⊞ 353
⊡ 504	

⊞ 3753	▦ 783
932	▦ 400
▦ 3364	⊞ 606
564	▦ 304
563	■ 915
■ 561	▦ 838
733	

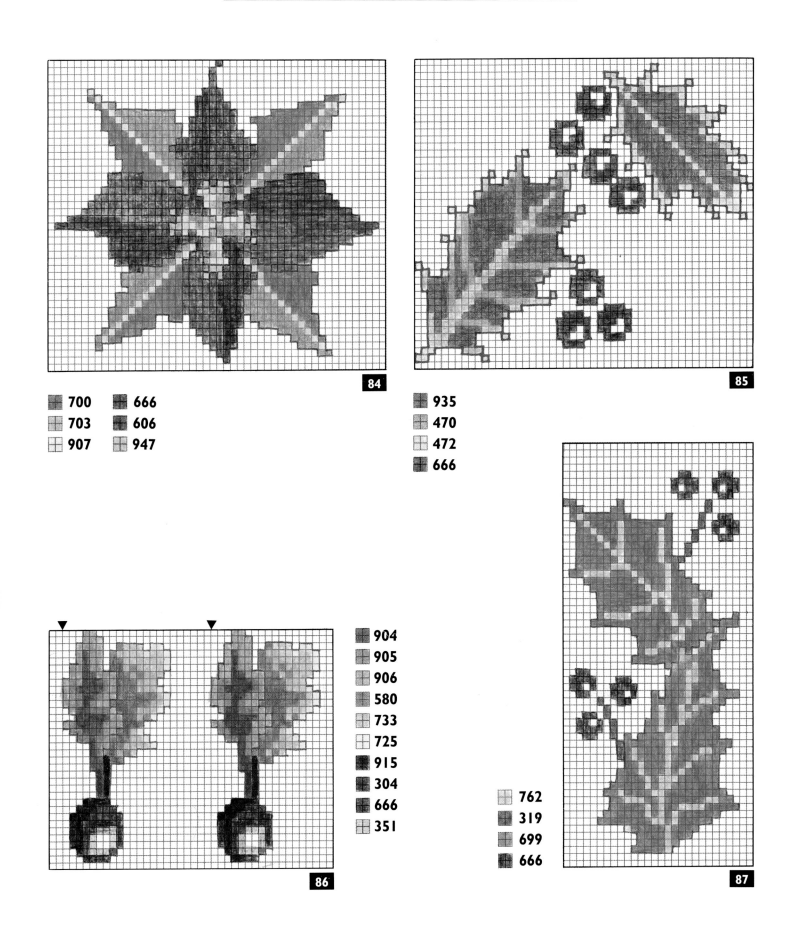

84

700		666	
703		606	
907		947	

85

935	
470	
472	
666	

86

904	
905	
906	
580	
733	
725	
915	
304	
666	
351	

87

762	
319	
699	
666	

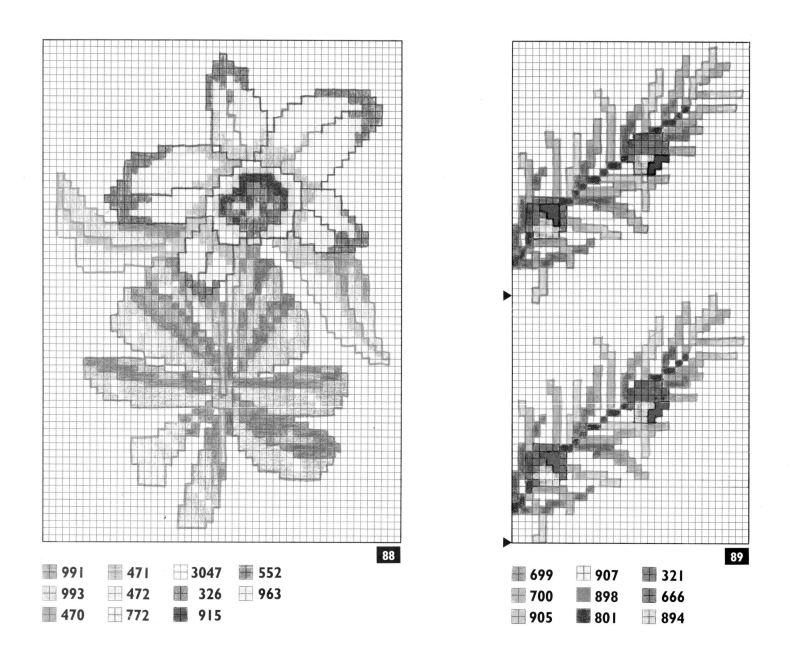

88

991	471	3047	552
993	472	326	963
470	772	915	

89

699	907	321
700	898	666
905	801	894

90

699	
701	
703	
433	
600	
666	
917	
754	

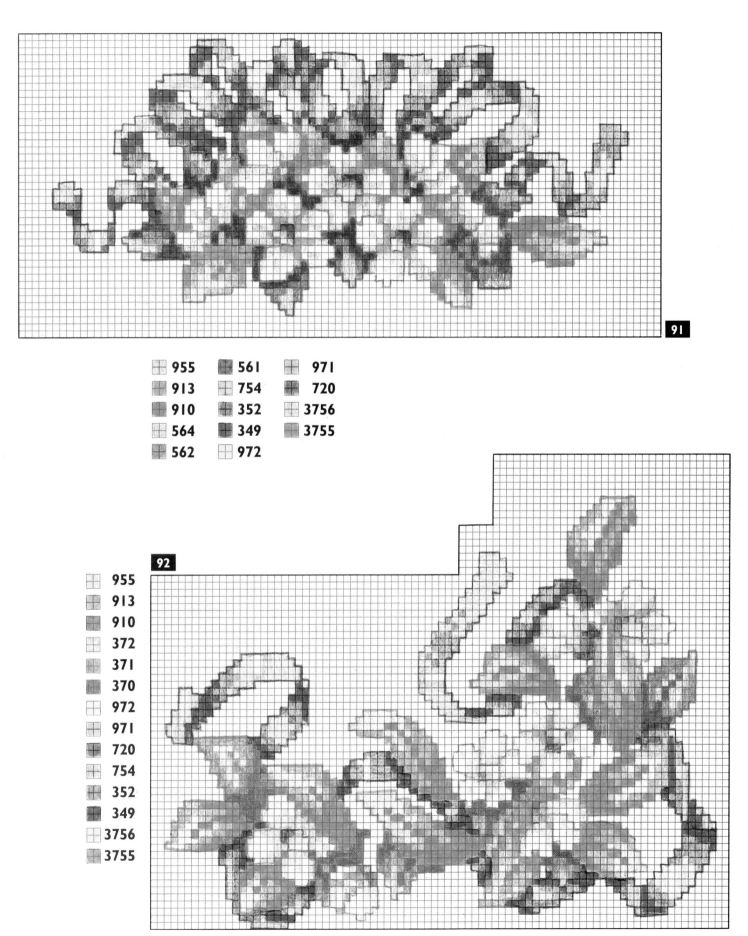

91

955	561	971
913	754	720
910	352	3756
564	349	3755
562	972	

92

955
913
910
372
371
370
972
971
720
754
352
349
3756
3755

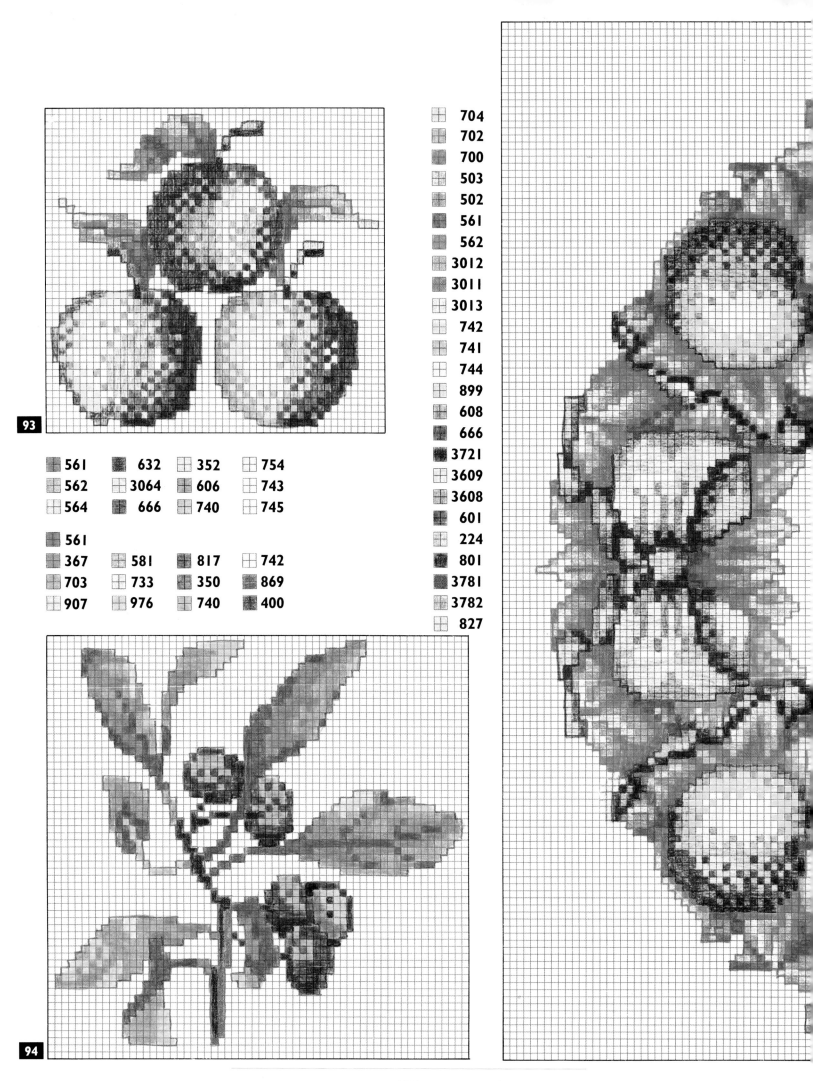

93

▦ 561	▦ 632	⊞ 352	⊞ 754
▦ 562	⊞ 3064	▦ 606	⊞ 743
⊞ 564	▦ 666	⊞ 740	⊞ 745

▦ 561			
▦ 367	▦ 581	▦ 817	⊞ 742
⊞ 703	⊞ 733	▦ 350	▦ 869
⊞ 907	⊞ 976	⊞ 740	▦ 400

⊞	704
⊞	702
▦	700
⊞	503
⊞	502
⊞	561
⊞	562
▦	3012
▦	3011
⊞	3013
⊞	742
⊞	741
⊞	744
⊞	899
⊞	608
⊞	666
▦	3721
⊞	3609
▦	3608
▦	601
⊞	224
▦	801
▦	3781
▦	3782
⊞	827

94

Inspirations in
GREEN

G reen, in embroidery, is often the color that complements or provides background. Leafy branches, foliage, and grass always make a good frame, whether in soft shades of green or stronger and more pronounced tones. This is because green highlights the red of a juniper berry, the rose of petals, and the yellow and orange of fruit and vegetables. The result of combining green with such colors is a totally natural, eye-pleasing, and reassuring contrast.

But green also makes a great dominant color that is calming, peaceful, and restful. The more vibrant shades of green provide a clarity that represents rebirth and springtime and reflects the hope and renewal of that season.

Even though vegetation is abundantly represented through the richness of green, nature has, at the same time, skillfully protected itself from too much interference from human endeavor. There are, for example, few green mineral substances from which pigments and dye can be obtained. The discovery of the shade known as "green jade of Scotland" is a rare exception. It was discovered centuries ago in a stone and was hailed as a milestone in dye-making research.

This wonderfully natural color surrounds us in grass and the leafy branches of trees, and provides its own fascinating world of fantasy—dragons, monsters, elves, and alien creatures are often represented in green. There is a similar magic in the "green flash" that sometimes lights up the Caribbean sky just before the sun sets on the day.

Few of us realize that green is also the color of the planet Venus, and in certain countries, by association, it was customary to dress in green for weddings, as Venus symbolized love.

𝒫ages 102–103: Three borders reminiscent of the geometric folk designs found in Greece, Russia, and the Great North. The folkloric designs often feature yellow and red, as well, but in the three borders presented here, green mixed with white predominates to provide a striking decorative effect. The borders, carefully positioned, can decorate a table napkin, a cushion, or a curtain. Begin the embroidery at one end, working on all three borders as you move between the edges of the frame. On the left, the close-up detail of the design shows that while it may appear complicated, it is, in fact, quite straightforward and simple whether worked horizontally or vertically.

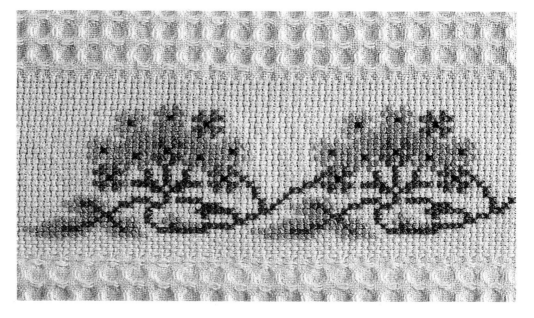

INSPIRATIONS IN GREEN

bove and left: A delightful, miniature garden adds life to a set of towels. The gracefulness of the tiny flowers with the gentle touch of green creates the delicate effect of Liberty lines in the design. The design is beautiful as a main feature but can also be worked as a border using the same colors but altering the shades of each mini-bouquet. This shading is very eye-catching on a curtain, quilt, or tablecloth.

On the 11-count Aida border, the motif will be about 2 in. in height. If you choose 11- or 14-count Aida, the same design will measure about 2 in. or 1½ in. in height, respectively.

*A*bove: Wreaths offer many variations. The designs complete a gift, a placemat, or a box. The two wreaths linked here with a pink ribbon can decorate a curtain or a sampler. The motif can also be used as a border. It will, however, be a fairly large border, as each wreath requires 46 stitches. The size of the wreath can be increased if, instead of working on every thread of the fabric edge, each cross stitch is embroidered over 2 threads, remembering to double the thread. (See p. 112.)

*R*ight: The yellow juniper berry evokes an impression of summer; red, of Christmas. For a look that is very refined, try coloring the berries blue or lilac and the leaves and branches in a darker shade. (See pp. 110 and 113.)

Inspirations in Green

THE DESIGNS

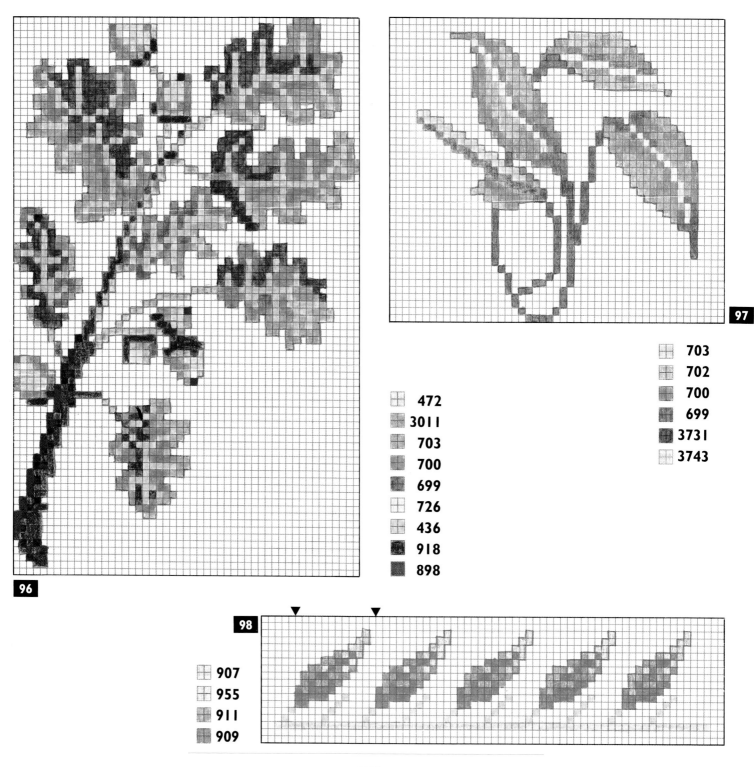

96

97

98

	472
	3011
	703
	700
	699
	726
	436
	918
	898

	703
	702
	700
	699
	3731
	3743

	907
	955
	911
	909

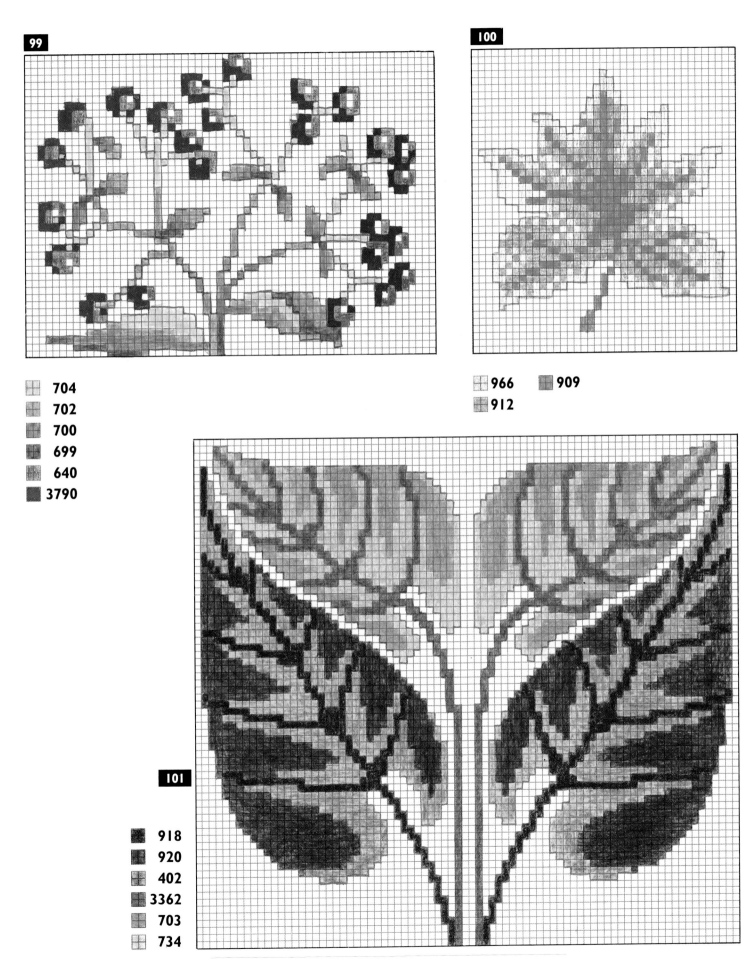

99

704
702
700
699
640
3790

100

966   909
912

101

918
920
402
3362
703
734

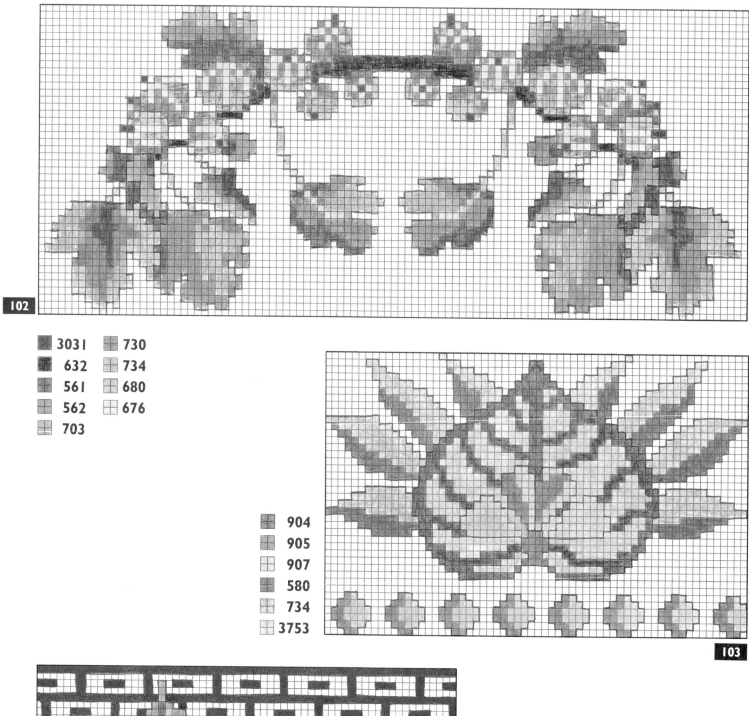

102

■ 3031	▦ 730
■ 632	▦ 734
▦ 561	▦ 680
▦ 562	▦ 676
▦ 703	

▦ 904	
▦ 905	
▦ 907	
▦ 580	
▦ 734	
▦ 3753	

103

104

■ 839	
▦ 700	
▦ 702	
▦ 704	
▦ 469	
▦ 472	
▦ 445	

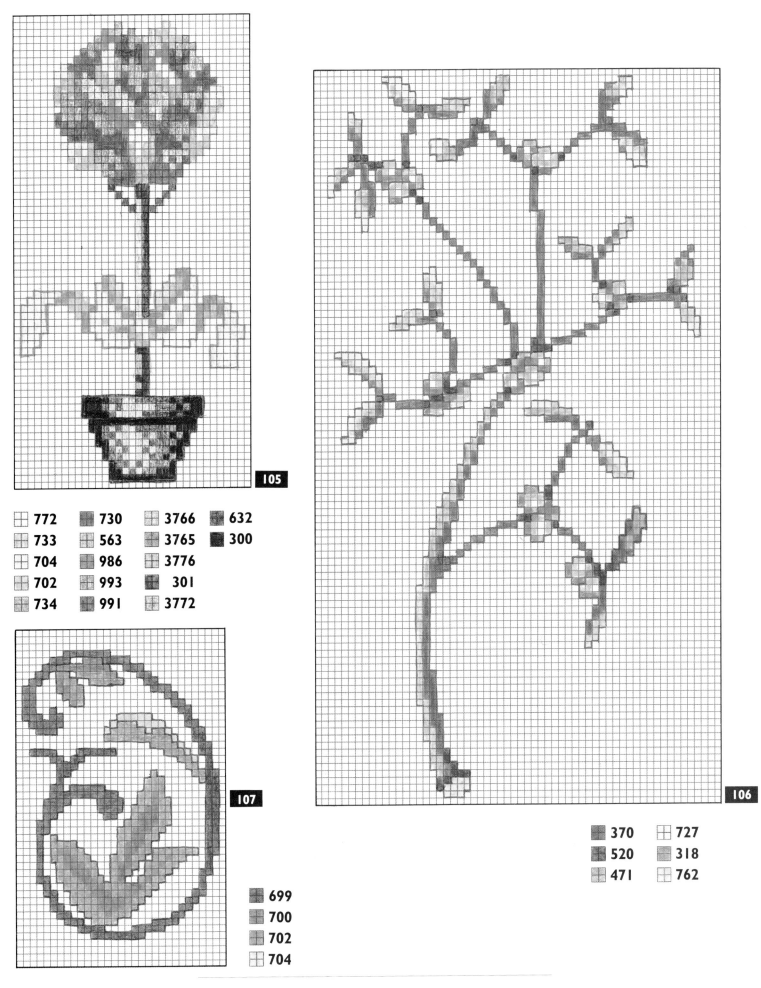

⊞ 772	▨ 730	⊞ 3766	▨ 632
▨ 733	⊞ 563	▨ 3765	▨ 300
⊞ 704	▨ 986	⊞ 3776	
▨ 702	▨ 993	▨ 301	
⊞ 734	▨ 991	⊞ 3772	

105

106

▨ 370	⊞ 727
▨ 520	▨ 318
⊞ 471	⊞ 762

107

▨ 699
▨ 700
▨ 702
⊞ 704

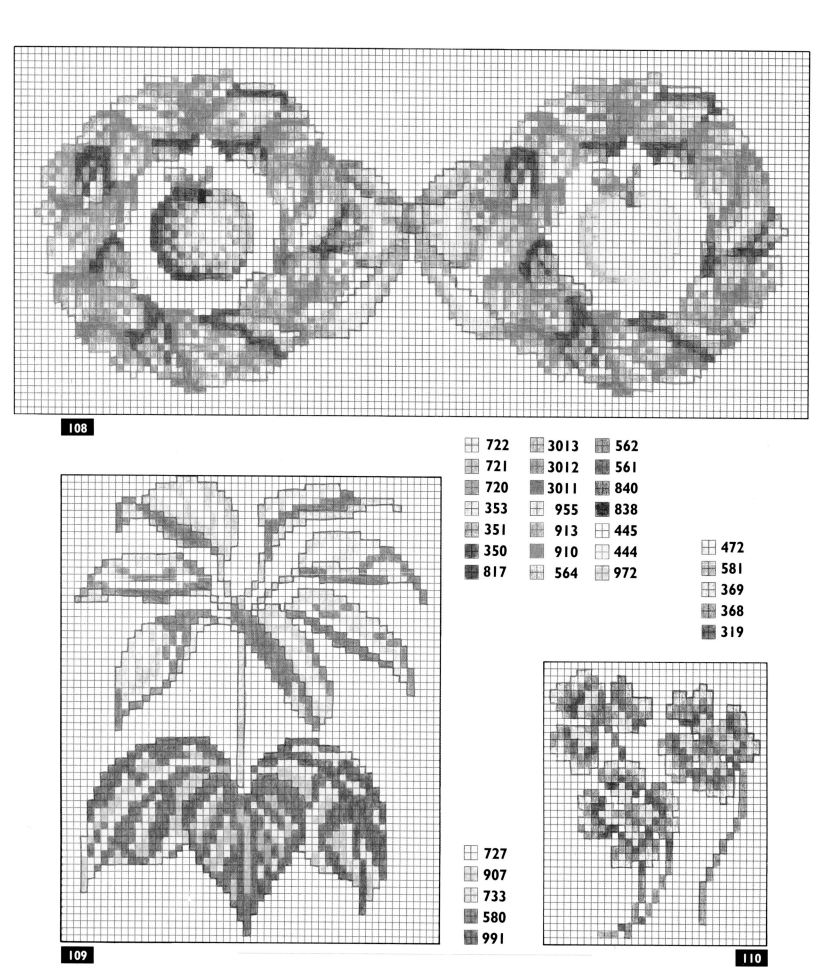

108

⊞ 722	⊞ 3013	⊞ 562
⊞ 721	⊞ 3012	⊞ 561
⊞ 720	▦ 3011	⊞ 840
⊞ 353	⊞ 955	■ 838
⊞ 351	▦ 913	⊞ 445
■ 350	▦ 910	⊞ 444
▦ 817	⊞ 564	⊞ 972

⊞ 472
⊞ 581
⊞ 369
⊞ 368
■ 319

⊞ 727
⊞ 907
⊞ 733
▦ 580
▦ 991

109

110

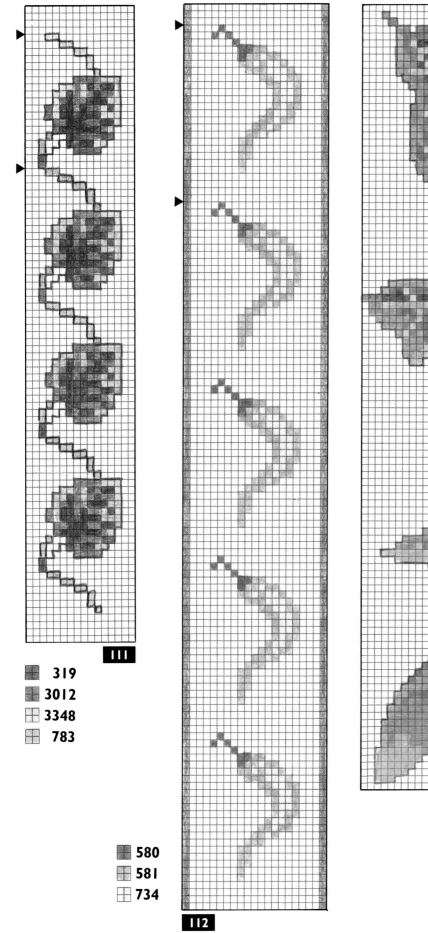

	319
	3012
	3348
	783

111

	580
	581
	734

112

113

	472		890		938
	701		783		608
	704		920		349
	699		780		

THE TECHNIQUE

*J*ust as it is necessary to know the alphabet in order to write, it is necessary with cross stitch to know the two simple, basic components of its composition—two oblique crossover lines. Throughout the world, we can trace a period in the history of nearly every country when cross stitch has been employed. Embroidered items include furniture in even the poorest of homes, linen, clothing, and drapery. Beginner's efforts, made by children learning to work with needle and thread, are kept as mementos of childhood.

In essence cross stitch is a simple stitch that does not require other stitches to enhance it. It is used on its own in designs with either a single color tone or a shaded color effect. The only accompanying stitch that is sometimes used is backstitch, useful for outlining the edges of a design, where a light colored thread is used on a light colored fabric, making it difficult to distinguish the design from the fabric. It is also used to emphasize a line of color.

An equivalent style used in the Umbrian district of Italy is known as the "Assisi Stitch." It is most often stitched in blue or rust colored thread and its usage originated in the town of Assisi. Cross stitch was used to fill the background of designs and a backstitch outline resulted in an effect that helped the central figures of the design, often birds or animals, to stand out quite prominently. Church decorations, monuments, signs, and buildings, as well as laying, bas-relief, wrought iron, and wood sculptures provided a vast repertoire which, in turn, offered an inexhaustible supply of motifs for embroidery designs.

The cross-stitch technique varies from country to country, and often, while maintaining the basic characteristics of the stitch, there are variations in the length of the stitch.

When cross stitch is used on canvas, the entire background design needs to be filled in so that the color of the canvas is not visible. This is not necessary on various other types of material, but above all, it is essential that the count and the weave of the fabric be even so that the crosses are identical in shape and size.

Once the motif has been chosen, it is important to plan the design on paper, especially if it is a complex one. You need to have the measurements in proportion in order to have a total picture of the finished design. Accurate measurements will help you to see any possible obstacles before you begin your work. Likewise, you should determine the size, both in length and width, of your chosen motif and then carefully tack the design onto the rectangle you have marked with colored thread. This way you will be able to see if the design is ornate enough for the tablecloth, if one border is sufficient decoration for a curtain, or whether a table runner would look better with a double border. Initial calculation of the amount of space needed, whether for letters of the alphabet or small motifs of fruit, is a vital first step. If such a precaution is taken, there will be no unpleasant surprises with the finished piece.

Corners for a border motif can easily be created using the following technique: place a mirror along the diagonal of the proposed corner so that the complete motif is reflected in the mirror. Copy this reflected image onto graph paper, stitch by stitch, before continuing into the embroidery stage. If the chosen motifs are printed in color only, and you experience difficulty in distinguishing the colors, carefully transform the design into a sketch in black and white using conventional symbols to represent the various colors.

With the actual embroidery, it is best to work on the design first with all the required colors and tones, leaving the completion of the background until this is finished. It is also wise to complete a whole flower or a face of an animal before starting on the next motif. This will highlight problems at an early stage and allow the positioning of all the motifs so that the design is not cluttered.

THE STITCHES

ross-stitch embroidery is an enjoyable technique. If the basic steps, which are few and uncomplicated, are followed, some incredible results can be achieved. For example, when working with a multicolored motif, take care with the wrong side of the fabric and keep the threads tidy. The threads at the back of work should never be left too long, and ends should be run back under the existing stitches on the reverse side of the fabric.

Backstitch must also be executed according to the instructions given in order to achieve a finished look that is aesthetically pleasing. Ideally, if you are working on a design in which the entire fabric needs to be filled in with cross stitch, work horizontally from left to right and vice versa. In cases where the outline is oblique,

make a border using a half-cross stitch. This stitch is formed using a slanting or diagonal stitch and a small stitch that is perpendicular to the long one but meets at its center.

When beginning or ending a thread, avoid the use of knots, as they will show through to the right side. (Also, frequent washing and the passage of time may cause the knots to come undone.) To begin stitching, leave a length of thread at the back of the fabric, then work several stitches to secure it. To finish off a thread, weave the end under the last few stitches on the reverse side of the fabric. This method will give the embroidery a finished look on both the front and back of the work and is ideal when working on curtains.

CROSS STITCH

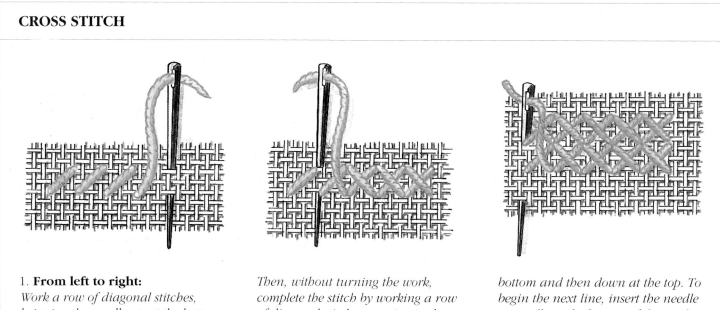

1. **From left to right:**
Work a row of diagonal stitches, bringing the needle up at the bottom of the stitch and then down at the top to complete the diagonal.

Then, without turning the work, complete the stitch by working a row of diagonal stitches: moving in the other direction over the top of the first row, bring the needle up at the

bottom and then down at the top. To begin the next line, insert the needle vertically at the bottom of the stitch. On the back of the work there will be a sequence of vertical stitches.

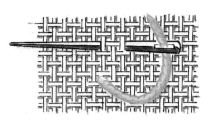

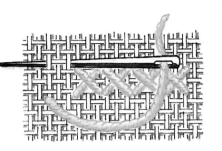

2. From right to left:
Work a diagonal stitch, bringing the needle up at the bottom of the stitch on the left and then inserting it diagonally to the right at the top

Complete the cross stitch by repeating the diagonal stitch in the other direction: bring the needle up at the top of the stitch on the left and then insert the needle diagonally to the right at the bottom.

Continue in this manner, but make sure that you leave enough space for the new stitch at the first step. Complete each stitch before proceeding to the next one.

3. From bottom to top:
Bring the needle up at the top and work in a diagonal direction to the

bottom left corner. Complete by working the diagonal stitch from the top left corner to the bottom right

corner, then moving to the next line in a vertical direction. Repeat the process for as many stitches as required.

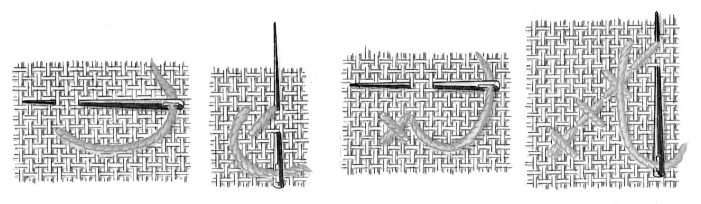

4. An upward diagonal direction:
Work the first complete cross as in step

2, but finish with the needle at the top right corner. Work the next cross stitch

in same manner in a diagonal direction to the right and up.

5. A downward diagonal direction:
Work the first cross as in step 3, but

finish with the needle at the bottom left corner. Work the next cross stitch in

the same manner, left and down, in the diagonal direction.

DOUBLE RUNNING STITCH

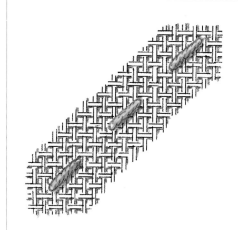

6. A straight line:
Work from right to left, making a row of evenly spaced stitches. Again

working from right to left, complete by working a second row, stitching in the spaces between the first row of stitches.

The result is a continuous line of stitches all the same size.

7. A diagonal line:
Beginning from the top right corner, work a row of stitches the same size,

on both sides of the fabric, moving diagonally to the bottom left. To complete, work a second row, again

moving diagonally from top right. The result is a continuous line of stitches all the same size.

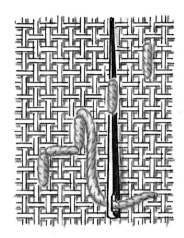

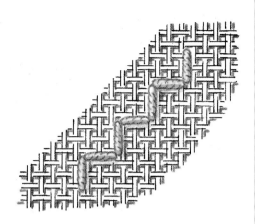

8. In a stepped manner:
Work a row of parallel, vertical lines, spaced so that a stitch the same size, in

both horizontal and vertical directions, can be placed between them. To finish, work a second row,

parallel and horizontal, between the vertical stitches. This row should be the same size as the vertical stitches.

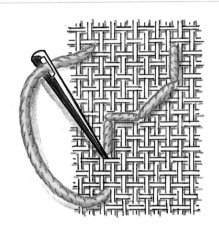

9. Backstitch for outlining:
Work stitches in any direction required to create a continuous line by bringing the thread up in front of the last stitch, leaving space for the new stitch, and then back into the fabric to fill in the space.

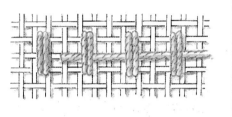

10. Beginning and finishing off a thread:
When you start stitching the first diagonals, make sure the thread end

is secured under the vertical stitch lines on the wrong side. To end, pass the thread under three or four of the double vertical stitches.

THE FABRICS

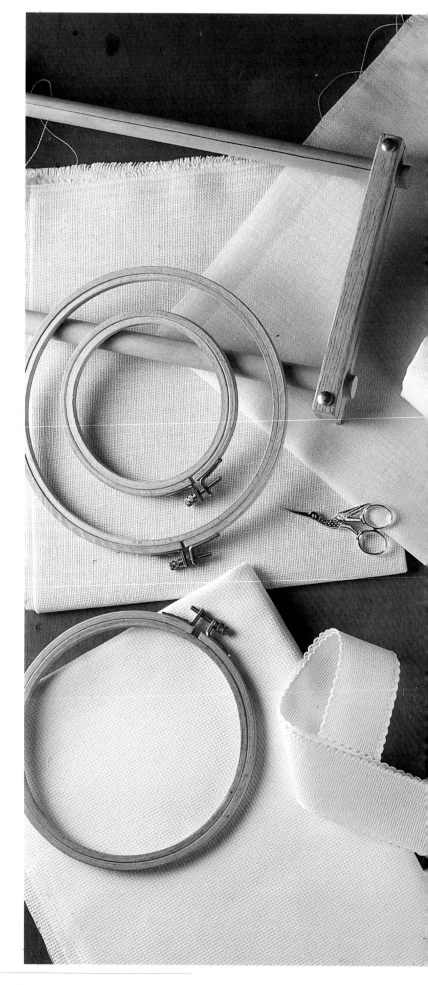

$\mathscr{A}$ fabric count is the number of threads per inch of fabric. For a perfect result, it is essential that it is absolutely even. The various kinds of Aida fabric are particularly good for cross stitch, as the fabric count and the weave combine to form perfect squares. Pure linen is also good, providing 18 to 40 threads per inch.

The Aida fabric in pure cotton is available in many widths, and the thread count varies from 6 to 18. The same motif, depending on the fabric, will require different measurements according to the thread count of the fabric. The smaller the thread count, the larger the finished design.

Pure linen with a regular fabric count suitable for cross stitch is also available in a variety of widths. It comes in white, unbleached, or colored forms and in thread counts from 18 to 40. Naturally the number of the stitches possible will lessen if the threads are larger. Even with Aida fabric, a 2 × 2 in. square measurement will give very different sizes and results. A word of advice: because of the delicate nature of cross-stitch designs, it is best to choose a fabric that will wear well with time and laundering. Bear in mind also that since pure cotton is as pleasing aesthetically as pure linen, it can also be considered when choosing a suitable fabric.

$\mathscr{L}$ inen and Aida fabric have an even thread count and lend themselves perfectly to cross stitch. The even thread count allows a needle to slide through the material effortlessly. Colored thread is likewise not a problem because the size of this thread is no thicker than the thread of the fabric. Obviously the dimensions of the embroidery vary depending on the type of fabric and the thread count, as can be seen with the rose design demonstrated on 14-, 18-, and 22-count Aida fabric with embroidery floss of 1, 2, and 3 threads.

THE THREADS

The DMC color chart is based on Stranded Floss and Perle Cotton colors, and there are 398 different shades from which to choose the perfect tone of color. There are at least eleven variations of each color.

When choosing a design, thread, or fabric, other factors must be considered for the result you envisage. A thicker thread, for example, will require a larger count in the fabric; a thinner thread will need a smaller count.

The DMC Stranded Floss and Perle Cotton have different features for the same color. Stranded Floss is soft, flexible, and luminous, comes in ready-made skeins, and is made up of six fine threads that are perfect for filling in the background fabric on a completed embroidery design. Because of the nature of its composition, this thread can be separated and used as 1-, 2-, 7-, or 10-thread thickness. In other words, its usage can be adapted to even the lightest fabric and to every design.

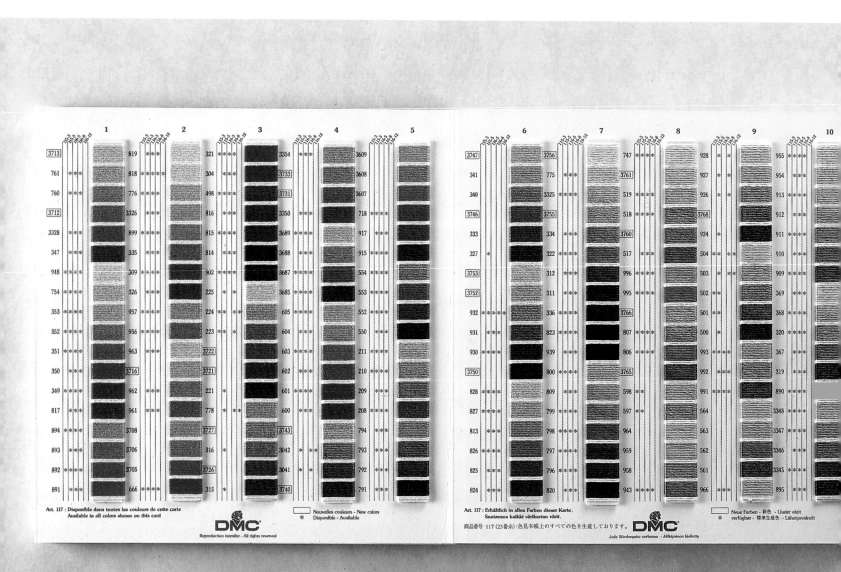

The DMC Perle Cotton, on the other hand, is a single shiny strand, available in balls or skeins. It comes in two varieties: Number 5 and Number 8. No. 8 Perle is recommended for single-color designs because the twist of the thread can help give a brighter, clearer look to the outline of the embroidered fabric. No. 5 Perle is suitable for embroidery on fabrics with a coarser count.

A final word of advice: whenever possible, it is always best to work on the darker colors of a design first, filling in the lighter colors last. This is because lighter shades seem to soil more readily and in so doing can spoil the overall effect of the finished design.

The entire range of embroidery threads available from DMC offers 398 varieties of combined and tinted shades. This broad choice should guarantee a tone that is just right for any design or piece of embroidery.

INSTRUCTIONS FOR THE DESIGNS

*C*hapter by chapter the pages of this book unfold from shades of rose to shades of green like the colors of the rainbow. Each color has inspirational photographs and examples of designs that have already been made up on paper grids. Also included is a number of designs shown only in chart form. These designs should help enrich your personal collection.

All the designs are numbered progressively throughout the book for easier identification. Below is a set of instructions for each one where the number of stitches both in width and height is given. The measurements are based on 11-, 14-, or 16-count Aida fabric. This information will help you to choose the best type of fabric and yarn for the design. The page reference at the end of any instruction refers specifically to either a photograph of an existing embroidery or one of the designs.

Inspirations in ROSE

1 The design is 95 stitches wide by 39 stitches high. If stitched on 11-count Aida, it is 8½ × 3½ in.; on 14- or 16-count Aida, the dimensions are roughly 6½ × 3 in. or 6½ × 2½ in. respectively.

2 The repeat motif indicated by the arrows is 28 stitches wide by 26 stitches high. It measures approximately 2 × 2 in., 2 × 1½ in., or 1½ × 1½ in. respectively on Aida of 11-, 14-, or 16-count.

3 The design repeat is 104 stitches high and 28 stitches wide. The measurements are approximately 9½ × 2½ in., 7½ × 2 in., or 7 × 1½ in. respectively on 11-, 14-, or 16-count Aida.

4 The design is 59 stitches wide by 47 stitches high.

Cross stitched on 11-, 14-, or 16-count Aida, it measures approximately 5 × 4½ in., 4½ × 3½ in., or 4 × 3 in. respectively.

5 The motif repeat is 35 × 35 stitches. On 11-, 14-, or 16-count Aida, it measures approximately 3 × 3 in., 2½ × 2½ in., or 2½ × 2½ in. respectively.

6 The motif repeat indicated by the arrows is 44 stitches across and 20 stitches high. On 11-, 14-, or 16-count Aida, it is approximately 4 × 1½ in., 3 × 1½ in., or 3 × 1½ in. respectively. (See photograph on p. 30.)

7 The design is 62 × 62 stitches. On 11-, 14-, or 16-count Aida, it is approximately 5½ × 5½ in., 4½ × 4½ in., or 4 × 4 in. respectively.

8 The design is 108 × 108 stitches. On Aida of 11-, 14-, or 16-count, it is approx-

imately 9½ × 9½ in., 8 × 8 in., or 7 × 7 in. respectively.

9 The design is 76 stitches wide and 72 stitches high. On 11-, 14-, or 16-count Aida, it is approximately 6½ × 6½ in., 5½ × 5 in., or 5 × 4½ in. respectively.

10 The repeat of the design between the arrows is 77 stitches across and 55 stitches high. On 11-, 14-, or 16-count Aida, it is approximately 7 × 5 in., 5½ × 4 in., or 5½ × 3½ in. respectively. (See photograph on p. 15.)

11 The repeat of the design between the arrows is 90 stitches high and 76 stitches across. On 11-, 14-, or 16-count Aida, it is approximately 8 × 6½ in., 6½ × 5½ in., or 6 × 5 in. respectively.

12 The motif repeat between the arrows is 31 stitches high and 25 stitches wide. On Aida of 11-, 14-,

or 16-count, it is approximately 3 × 2 in., 2 × 1½ in., or 2 × 1½ in. respectively.

13 The design is 192 stitches wide and 131 stitches high. On 11-, 14-, or 16-count Aida, it is approximately 17 × 12 in., 14 × 9½ in., or 12½ × 8½ in. respectively. (See photograph on p. 14.)

Inspirations in BLUE

14 The design is 80 × 82 stitches. On 11-, 14-, or 16-count Aida, it is approximately 7 × 7½ in., 5½ × 6 in., or 5½ × 5½ in. respectively. (See photograph on p. 29.)

15 The motif repeat between the arrows is 27 stitches across and 25 stitches high. On Aida of 11-, 14-, or 16-count, it is approximately 2½ × 2 in., 2 × 1½ in., or 1½ × 1½ in. respectively.

16 The design is 61 stitches across and 73 stitches high. On 11-, 14-, or 16-count Aida, it is approximately 5½ × 6½ in., 4½ × 5½ in., or 4 × 5 in. respectively.

17 The design is 102 × 102 stitches and on the above-mentioned fabrics, it measures approximately 9 × 9 in., 7½ × 7½ in., or 6½ × 6½ in. respectively.

18 The design is 53 × 64 stitches and it measures approximately 4½ × 5½ in., 3½ × 4½ in., or 3½ × 4 in. respectively.

19 The design is 24 × 49 stitches and it measures approximately 2 × 3½ in., 1½ × 3½ in., or 1½ × 3 in. respectively.

20 The motif repeat is 24 × 33 stitches and it measures approximately 2 × 3 in., 1½ × 2½ in., or 1½ × 2 in. respectively.

21 The design is 45 × 58 stitches and it measures approximately 4 × 5 in., 3 × 4 in., or 3 × 3½ in. respectively.

22 The design is 104 × 79 stitches and it measures approximately 9½ × 7 in., 7½ × 5½ in., or 7 × 5 in. respectively.

23 The design repeat is 27 stitches wide and 38 stitches high. It measures approximately 2½ × 3½ in., 2 × 3 in., or 1½ × 2½ in. respectively.

24 The design is 70 × 71 stitches and it measures approximately 6½ × 6½ in., 5 × 5 in., or 4½ × 4½ in. respectively.

25 The design is 19 stitches across and the repeat is 13 stitches high. It measures approximately 1½ × 1 in., 1½ × 1 in., or 1 × 1 in. respectively.

26 The design has a repeat of 99 stitches across and is 30 stitches high. It measures approximately 9 × 2½ in., 7 × 2 in., or 6½ × 2 in. respectively. (See photograph on p. 29.)

27 The design has a repeat of 56 stitches across and is 53 stitches high. It measures approximately 5 × 4½ in., 4 × 3½ in., or 3½ × 3½ in. respectively.

28 The design is 37 × 29 stitches and it measures approximately 3½ × 2½ in., 3 × 2½ in., or 2½ × 2 in. respectively.

29 The design has a repeat of 24 stitches across and is 33 stitches high. It measures approximately 2 × 3 in., 1½ × 2½ in., or 1½ × 2 in. respectively.

30 The design has a repeat of 27 stitches high and 42 stitches across. It measures approximately 2½ × 4 in., 2 × 3 in., or 1½ × 3 in. respectively.

31 The design has a repeat of 48 stitches across and is 32 stitches high. It measures approximately 4½ × 3 in., 3½ × 2½ in., or 3 × 2 in. respectively.

32 The design repeat is 9 stitches wide and is 5 stitches high. It measures approximately ½ in. on all three counts of fabric.

33 The design repeat is 48 × 40 stitches and measures approximately 4½ × 4 in., 3½ × 3 in., or 3 × 2½ in. respectively.

34 The design is 38 × 49 stitches and it measures approximately 3½ × 4½ in., 3 × 3½ in., or 2½ × 3 in. respectively.

35 The design is 31 × 52 stitches and it measures approximately 3 × 5 in., 2 × 3½ in., or 2 × 3½ in. respectively.

36 The design repeat is 44 stitches across and is 52 stitches high. It measures approximately 4 × 4½ in., 3 × 3½ in., or 3 × 3½ in. respectively.

37 The design repeat is 13 stitches across and is 22 stitches high. It measures approximately 1 × 2 in., 1 × 1½ in., or 1 × 1½ in. respectively.

38 The design is 33 stitches high and the repeat is 30 stitches across. It measures approximately 3 × 3 in., 2½ × 2 in., or 2 × 2 in. respectively.

39 The design is 62 × 34 stitches and it measures approximately 5½ × 3 in., 4½ × 2½ in., or 4 × 2 in. respectively.

40 The design is 137 × 136 stitches and it measures approximately 12 × 12 in., 8½ × 8½ in., or 5 × 5 in. respectively. (See photograph on p. 28.)

41 The design is 203 × 150 stitches and it measures approximately 18 × 13½ in., 14½ × 10½ in., or 13½ × 10 in. respectively. (See photograph on pp. 32–33.)

42 The design is 25 stitches wide and the repeat is 33

stitches high. It measures approximately 2 × 3 in., 1½ × 2½ in., or 1½ × 2 in. respectively.

Inspirations in
VIOLET

43 The design is 17 stitches across and the repeat is 16 stitches high. It measures approximately 1½ × 1½ in., 1 × 1 in., or 1 × 1 in. respectively

44 The design is 59 stitches wide and 93 stitches high. It measures approximately 5½ × 8½ in., 4½ × 6½ in., or 4 × 6 in. respectively.

45 The design repeat is 43 stitches wide and 40 stitches high. It measures approximately 4 × 3½ in., 3 × 3 in., or 3 × 2½ in. respectively.

46 The design is 17 stitches across and the repeat is 26 stitches high. It measures approximately 1½ × 2½ in., 1 × 2 in., or 1 × 1½ in. respectively.

47 The design (to be turned and repeated 4 times to complete the wreath) is 74 stitches wide and 78 stitches high. It measures approximately 13 × 14 in., 10½ × 11 in., or 9½ × 10 in. respectively. (See photograph on page 114.)

48 The design repeat is 38 × 38 stitches and it measures approximately 3½ × 3½ in., 3 × 3 in., or 2½ × 2½ in. respectively

49 The design repeat is 58 × 58 stitches and it measures approximately 5 × 5 in., 4 × 4 in., or 3½ × 3½ in. respectively.

50 The design is 103 stitches wide and 57 stitches high. It measures approximately 9½ × 5 in., 7½ × 4 in., or 6½ × 3½ in. respectively.

51 The design is 31 stitches across and 72 stitches high. It measures approximately 3 × 6½ in., 2 × 5 in., or 2 × 4½ in. respectively.

52 The design is 50 stitches across and 44 stitches high. It measures approximately 4½ × 4 in., 3½ × 3 in., or 3½ × 3 in. respectively.

53 The design repeat is 39 stitches high and is 31 stitches across. It measures approximately 3½ × 3 in., 3 × 2 in., or 2½ × 2 in. respectively.

54 The design is 142 × 142 stitches and it measures approximately 12 × 12 in., 6½ × 6½ in., or 5½ × 5½ in. respectively.

55 The design is 39 stitches across and 62 stitches high. It measures approximately 3½ × 5½ in., 3 × 4½ in., or 2½ × 4 in. respectively.

Inspirations in
YELLOW

56 The design repeat is 32 stitches across and 48 stitches high. It measures approximately 3 × 4½ in., 2½ × 3½ in., or 2 × 3 in. respectively. (See photograph on pp. 60–61.)

57 The design is 64 stitches across and 28 stitches high. It measures approximately 5½ × 2½ in., 4½ × 2 in., or 4 × 1½ in. respectively.

58 The design is 43 stitches across and 60 stitches high. It measures approximately 4 × 5½ in., 3 × 4½ in., or 3 × 4 in. respectively.

59 The design is 102 stitches wide and 110 stitches high. It measures approximately 9 × 10 in., 7½ × 8 in., or 6½ × 7½ in. respectively. (See photograph on pp. 62–63.)

60 The design repeat is 44 stitches wide and 39 stitches high. It measures approximately 4 × 3½ in., 3 × 3 in., or 3 × 2½ in. respectively.

61 The design repeat is 25 stitches across and 16 stitches high. It measures approximately 2 × 1½ in., 1½ × 1 in., or 1½ × 1 in. respectively.

62 The design repeat is 64 × 32 stitches and it measures approximately 5½ × 3 in., 4½ × 2½ in., or 4 × 2 in. respectively.

63 The design repeat is 49 × 39 stitches and it measures approximately 4½ × 3½ in., 3½ × 3 in., or 3 × 2½ in. respectively.

64 The design is 40 × 64 stitches and it measures approximately 3½ × 5½ in., 3 × 4½ in., or 2½ × 4 in. respectively.

65 The design is 52 × 52 stitches and it measures approximately 5 × 5 in., 3½ × 3½ in., or 3½ × 3½ in.

respectively.

66 The design is 180 × 140 stitches and it measures approximately 16 × 12½ in., 13 × 10 in., or 12 × 9½ in. respectively. (See photographs on pp. 64 and 65.)

Inspirations in
ORANGE

67 The design repeat is 18 × 32 stitches and it measures approximately 1½ × 3 in., 1½ × 2½ in., or 1 × 2 in. respectively.

68 The design is 61 stitches across and 102 stitches high. It measures approximately 5½ × 9 in., 4½ × 7½ in., or 4 × 6½ in. respectively.

69 The design repeat is 29 × 44 stitches and it measures approximately 2½ × 4 in., 2 × 3½ in., or 2 × 3 in. respectively.

70 The design repeat is 51 × 35 stitches and it measures approximately 4½ × 3 in., 3½ × 2½ in., or 3½ × 2½ in. respectively.

71 The design repeat is 15 × 16 stitches and it measures approximately 1½ × 1½ in., 1 × 1 in., or 1 × 1 in. respectively.

72 The design is 75 × 73 stitches and it measures approximately 6½ × 6½ in., 5½ × 5 in., or 5 × 4½ in. respectively. (See photograph on pp. 74–75.)

73 The design is 69 × 55 stitches and it measures approximately 6 × 5 in., 5

× 4 in., or 4½ × 3½ in. respectively. (See photograph on pp. 74–75.)

74 The design repeat is 26 × 31 stitches and it measures approximately 2½ × 3 in., 2 × 2 in., or 1½ × 2 in. respectively. (See photograph on p. 81.)

75 The design repeat is 19 × 11 stitches and it measures approximately 1½ × 1 in., 1½ × 1 in., or 1 × ½ in. respectively.

76 The design repeat is 31 × 77 stitches and it measures approximately 3 × 7 in., 2 × 5½ in., or 2 × 5½ in. respectively.

77 The design is 69 × 58 stitches and it measures approximately 6½ × 5 in., 5 × 4 in., or 4½ × 3½ in. respectively. (See photograph on p. 80.)

78 The design is 33 × 53 stitches and it measures approximately 3 × 4½ in., 2½ × 3½ in., or 2 × 3½ in. respectively. (See photograph on p. 80.)

79 The design repeat is 48 × 31 stitches and it measures approximately 4½ × 3 in., 3½ × 2 in., or 3 × 2 in. respectively.

80 The design is 26 × 41 stitches and it measures approximately 2½ × 3½ in., 1½ × 3 in., or 1½ × 3 in. respectively.

81 The design is 70 × 146 stitches and it measures approximately 6½ × 13 in., 5 × 12½ in., or 4½ × 9½ in. respectively. (See photographs on pp. 78 and 79.)

82 The design is 76 × 89 stitches and it measures approximately 6½ × 8 in., 5½ × 6½ in., or 5 × 6 in. respectively. (See photograph on p. 90.)

83 The design is 29 × 52 stitches and it measures approximately 2½ × 4½ in., 2 × 3½ in., or 2 × 3½ in. respectively.

84 The design is 48 × 43 stitches and it measures approximately 4½ × 4 in., 3½ × 3 in., or 3 × 3 in. respectively.

85 The design is 50 × 42 stitches and it measures approximately 4½ × 3½ in., 3½ × 3 in., or 3 × 3 in. respectively.

86 The design repeat is 22 × 33 stitches and it measures approximately 2 × 3 in., 1½ × 2½ in., or 1½ × 2 in. respectively.

87 The design is 26 × 54 stitches and it measures approximately 2½ × 5 in., 2 × 4 in., or 1½ × 3½ in. respectively.

88 The design is 49 × 67 stitches and it measures approximately 4½ × 6 in., 3½ × 4½ in., or 3 × 4½ in. respectively. (See photograph on p. 15.)

89 The design repeat is 34 × 35 stitches and it measures approximately 3 × 3 in., 2½ × 2½ in., or 2 × 2½

in. respectively.

90 The design repeat is 30 × 28 stitches and it measures approximately 2½ × 2 in., 2 × 2 in., or 2 × 1½ in. respectively. (See photograph on pp. 88–89.)

91 The design is 84 × 38 stitches and it measures approximately 7½ × 3½ in., 6 × 3 in., or 5½ × 2½ in. respectively. (See photograph on p. 91.)

92 The design is 81 × 61 stitches and it measures approximately 7½ × 5½ in., 6 × 4½ in., or 5½ × 4 in. respectively. (See photograph on p. 91.)

93 The design is 48 × 44 stitches and it measures 4½ × 4 in., 3½ × 3 in., or 3 × 3 in. respectively.

94 The design is 60 × 57 stitches and it measures approximately 5½ × 5 in., 4½ × 4 in., or 4 × 3½ in. respectively.

95 The design is 146 × 150 stitches and it measures approximately 12½ × 13 in., 10½ × 11 in., or 5½ × 6 in. respectively. (See photographs on pp. 92 and 93.)

96 The design is 51 × 78 stitches and it measures approximately 4½ × 7 in., 3½ × 5½ in., or 3½ × 5½ in. respectively.

97 The design is 41 × 41 stitches and it measures

approximately 3½ × 3½ in., 3 × 3 in., or 3 × 3 in. respectively.

98 The design repeat is 12 × 14 stitches and it measures approximately 1 × 1½ in. on all three counts of fabric.

99 The design is 55 × 43 stitches and it measures approximately 5 × 4 in., 4 × 3 in., or 3½ × 3 in. respectively.

100 The design is 37 × 37 stitches and it measures approximately 3½ × 3½ in., 2½ × 2½ in., or 2½ × 2½ in. respectively.

101 The design is 78 × 71 stitches and it measures approximately 7 × 6½ in., 5½ × 5 in., or 5 × 4½ in. respectively.

102 The design is 104 × 44 stitches and it measures approximately 9½ × 4 in., 7 × 3 in., or 7 × 3 in. respectively. (See photograph on p. 107.)

103 The design is 62 × 40 stitches and it measures approximately 5½ × 3½ in., 4½ × 3 in., or 4 × 2½ in. respectively.

104 The design is 62 × 41 stitches and it measures approximately 5½ × 3½ in., 4½ × 3 in., or 4 × 3 in. respectively.

105 The design is 33 × 65 stitches and it measures approximately 3 × 6 in., 2½ × 5 in., or 2 × 4½ in. respectively.

106 The design is 55 × 102 stitches and it measures

approximately 5 × 9 in., 4 × 7½ in., or 3½ × 6½ in. respectively.

107 The design is 29 × 41 stitches and it measures approximately 2½ × 3½ in., 2 × 3 in., or 2 × 3 in. respectively.

108 The design is 110 × 46 stitches and it measures approximately 10 × 4 in., 8 × 3½ in., or 7½ × 3 in. respectively. (See photograph on p. 106.)

109 The design is 52 × 65 stitches and it measures approximately 4½ × 6 in., 3½ × 4½ in., or 3½ × 4½ in. respectively.

110 The design is 31 × 39 stitches and it measures approximately 3 × 3½ in., 2 × 3 in., or 2 × 2½ in. respectively.

111 The design repeat is 12 × 19 stitches and it measures approximately 1 × 1½ in., 1 × 1½ in., or 1 × 1 in. respectively.

112 The design repeat is 21 × 25 stitches and it measures approximately 2 × 2 in., 1½ × 1½ in., or 1½ × 1½ in. respectively.

113 The design measures 55 × 109 stitches and it measures approximately 5 × 10 in., 4 × 8 in., or 3½ × 7 in. respectively. (See photograph on p. 107.)

·c　　　　　　．rned
shown below. Fines on
ue on a weekly basis or part thereof.

a